Step by Step
to College and Career Success

Third Edition

Step by Step
to College and Career Success

John N. Gardner
Distinguished Professor Emeritus, Library and
Information Science
Senior Fellow, National Resource Center for the First-Year
Experience and Students in Transition
University of South Carolina–Columbia

Executive Director, Policy Center on the First Year of College
Brevard, North Carolina

Betsy O. Barefoot
Codirector and Senior Scholar
Policy Center on the First Year of College
Brevard, North Carolina

BEDFORD/ST. MARTIN'S
Boston ◆ New York

For Bedford/St. Martin's

Executive Editor: Carrie Brandon
Developmental Editor: Julie Kelly
Production Editor: Kerri A. Cardone
Senior Production Supervisor: Dennis J. Conroy
Marketing Manager: Casey Carroll
Editorial Assistants: Sarah Guariglia and Nicholas Murphy
Copyeditor: Janet Gokay
Text Design: Brian Salisbury
Cover Art and Design: Sara Gates
Composition: Pre-Press PMG
Printing and Binding: R R Donnelley & Sons

President: Joan E. Feinberg
Editorial Director: Denise B. Wydra
Director of Marketing: Karen R. Soeltz
Director of Editing, Design, and Production: Marcia Cohen
Assistant Director of Editing, Design, and Production: Elise S. Kaiser
Managing Editor: Elizabeth M. Schaaf

Library of Congress Control Number: 2008935058

Manufactured in the United States of America.

3 2 1 0 9 8
f e d c b a

For information, write: Bedford/St. Martin's, 75 Arlington Street,
Boston, MA 02116   (617-399-4000)

ISBN-10:   0-312-68306-5
ISBN-13:   978-0-312-68306-1

Brief Contents

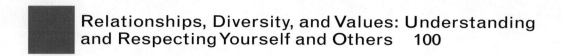
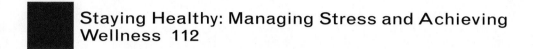
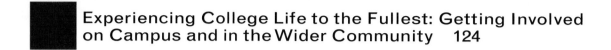

Contents

Staying Healthy: Managing Stress and Achieving Wellness 112

Experiencing College Life to the Fullest: Getting Involved on Campus and in the Wider Community 124

Making the Right Choices for Your Major and Career: Planning Early and Keeping an Open Mind 136

Preface

What does it mean to be a successful college student? Because today's students are more varied than ever before in terms of backgrounds, goals, and resources, the answer isn't always obvious.

Many students in college are seeking not only high academic performance but also practical tools for career advancement—or help succeeding at the jobs they have right now. Students at community colleges may plan to transfer to four-year schools, or they may be working toward an associate's degree or certificate. They may attend college full-time or part-time, in a string of continuous years or sporadically, as time and resources permit. At both four-year and two-year institutions, many more students today are "nontraditional," whether that means not fresh out of high school, older, or balancing the responsibilities of work and family care with the demands of school. Students with diagnosed or undiagnosed learning disabilities are increasingly mainstreamed into the educational system. We have more "Generation 1.5" students in our classrooms, who may speak English but who are more fluent in another language, or who may not be fluent in written, academic English. And many students today are the first in their families to attend college—so they may be particularly unfamiliar with the conventions of higher education in the U.S.

Given this variety of students and goals, there may not be a single definition of college success—but clearly, there's a greater need than ever for a course and a text that can support students and teachers in the college success course.

We created *Step by Step* to provide an accessible book that would be useful to all students, whatever their backgrounds or their college goals. We've pared away extras and have focused on the most crucial skills and the most important choices that students have to make. The scope of this book was not based solely on our own experience as college teachers: nationwide research continues to show that students are most likely to succeed if they follow the twelve steps covered here.

Along with the coverage, the tone, structure, and format of the book are carefully designed to engage all students and help them on their way to becoming successful and self-directed learners—and to make the book a useful resource in the classroom. Here are what we consider to be the key features of *Step by Step*.

Accessible and Easy to Use

Every sentence and paragraph has been edited with care to ensure that it is concise and to the point. The book's design is similarly streamlined and functional: each major topic begins with a large, bold heading on the left-hand page and is concluded by the end of the facing page. This modular organization not only makes the book easier for students to read, but it also helps them use the book as a reference, when they have a specific question. Smaller headings help signpost the material for students, and tips and guidelines are formatted as easy-to-find lists. Color coding and a system of tabs are used to distinguish the Steps—and to eliminate any sense that the Steps have to be assigned, read, or achieved in a lock-step fashion, we've removed the step numbers in the current edition.

An Active-Learning Approach that Culminates in Application

To help students put theory into practice; succinct lists give straightforward advice for every topic, from evaluating internet sources to maintaining friendships. Throughout the book, Try It! activities suggest ways students can immediately experiment with the skills and concepts in the chapters. Every Step concludes with a full-page worksheet that students can use to "take the next step" and apply the lessons to their actual situations, in a meaningful way. And to help students take more control of their own success, every chapter includes a quick overview of further resources for support, including learning assistance centers, books, Web sites, and fellow students—with a prompt for students to add their own ideas.

A Concrete Focus on Personal Goals, Learning Objectives, and Self-Assessment

Students need a clear sense of where they stand and what progress they're making. We've created a set of features that make this clear to students—and that can also be used by teachers for assessment and to guide instructional decisions. The first Step sets the stage by asking students to identify their goals and make a commitment to college success. Then, at the beginning of each Step throughout the book, students read the learning objectives for the Step and take a simple quiz to see how they measure up. At the end of the Step, students give themselves a post-test by listing key things they have learned and can start using immediately.

Ongoing Emphasis on Career and Workplace As Well As College

Students today are more career focused than ever, and are more likely than ever to be working in addition to attending school. Very likely, the success they're most focused on is success in their current and future jobs. Fortunately, the steps for success that we focus on in this textbook can as easily be applied to the workplace as to college: every Step concludes with a brief section pointing out how the lessons of the chapter also apply to the career and workplace. In addition to this, we include a meaty section on Finding a Job while still a student and our final Step is wholly devoted to Making the Right Choices for Your Major and Career.

Attention to the Growing Role Technology Plays in Success

Even techno-savvy students may not be making the most of their technology tools. New to this edition, easy-to-find Wired Window boxes throughout the book give students advice on topics such as taking notes on a laptop computer, taking exams on a course management system, maintaining online profiles that are appropriate for potential employers, and avoiding plagiarism when researching online. Because technology is deeply woven into students' lives, not a separate topic to them, we've also included technology-related coverage in the main text where appropriate, including for example the topics of Critically Evaluating Information on the Internet and Preparing for a Career in the Information Economy.

Research Based and Up to Date

As described above, this book represents not only the practical experience of our extensive careers teaching and directing this course but also the culmination of decades of research, disseminated through two national higher education centers which we have founded and directed. Although we don't trumpet this fact to students, every piece of advice and every statistic is grounded in the most up-to-date research possible. And the range of specific topics covered reflects what we hear in our ongoing conversations with instructors around the country. For example, in response to your requests, in this edition we have added coverage on classroom etiquette and civility, and we've expanded the discussion of Embracing Campus Diversity to encompass diversity in terms of age, learning and physical abilities, and sexual orientation.

Teaching Aids for Instructors

Instructor's Manual and Test Bank

The Instructor's Manual and Test Bank includes chapter objectives, teaching suggestions, additional exercises, test questions, a list of common concerns of first-year students, an introduction to the first-year experience course, a sample lesson plan for each chapter, and various case studies relevant to the topics covered. ISBN-10: 0-312-68308-1; ISBN-13: 978-0-312-68308-5

VideoCentral

VideoCentral is a growing collection of videos for the college success classroom. Meet academic, real world, and student writers and listen to tips on writing for the classroom and life. Hear from real students discussing their own experiences transitioning to college life. Coming fall 2009.

Student Resources

Step by Step Student Central

Web site bedfordstmartins.com/stepbystep offers a variety of rich learning resources designed to enhance the student experience. These resources include video tips from real students, self-awareness exercises to assess your students' strengths and weaknesses, Quick Guides to refresh basic skills in grammar, writing and reading, downloadable podcasts for quick study tips, and more.

The Bedford/St. Martin's Planner with Grammar Girl's Quick and Dirty Tips

Includes everything that students need to plan and use their time effectively, with advice on preparing schedules and to-do lists and blank schedules and calendars (monthly and weekly) for planning. Integrated into the planner are tips from the popular Grammar Girl podcast (and from other podcast hosts); quick advice on fixing common grammar errors, note-taking, and succeeding on tests; an address book; and an annotated list of useful Web sites. The planner fits easily into a backpack or purse, so students can take it anywhere. ISBN-10: 0-312-48023-7; ISBN-13: 978-0-312-48023-3

Acknowledgments

Although this text speaks with the voices of its two authors, it represents contributions from many others. We gratefully acknowledge those contributions and thank these individuals, whose special expertise has made it possible to introduce new college students to their college experience through the holistic approach we deeply believe in:

Michelle Murphy Burcin, *University of South Carolina at Columbia*

Tom Carskadon, *Mississippi State University*

James B. Craig, *University of California, Irvine*

Juan Flores, *Folsom Lake College*

Philip Gardner, *Michigan State University*

Jeanne L. Higbee, *University of Minnesota, Twin Cities*

Mary Ellen O'Leary, *University of South Carolina at Columbia*

Constance Staley, *University of Colorado at Colorado Springs*

R. Stephen Staley, *Colorado Technical University*

John M. Whiteley, *University of California, Irvine*

Edward Zlotkowski, *Bentley College*

Special thanks goes to Julie Alexander of the Policy Center on the First Year of College, for providing our Building Your Portfolio additions and Rey Junco of Lockhaven University of Pennsylvania, for his thoughtful work on the Wired Window feature.

We are also indebted to the following reviewers who offered us thoughtful and constructive feedback on the book:

Eunie Alsaker, *Winona State University*

Andrés Armijo, *University of New Mexico*

Marianne Auten, *Paradise Valley Community College*

Marlene Ballejos, *University of New Mexico*

Rob Burford, *University of New Mexico*

Kathleen A. Gover, *Brooklyn College*

Jennifer L. Crissman Ishler, *Pennsylvania State University*

Robert Peeler, *Lamar State College*

Sherri Anna Robinson, *North Virginia Community College*

Bruce Skolnick, *Edinboro University of Pennsylvania*

Finally, life is full of expected and unexpected changes including in the world of college text publishing. When we started our work on this edition, it was to have been published by Cengage Learning. However, during the production period, an outstanding college text publisher, Bedford/St. Martin's, acquired our titles. We respect and appreciate the contributions of our former Cengage team in helping us reach and assist hundreds of thousands of new college students. As we look to the future, we are excited about the contributions the Bedford/St. Martin's team will make to improve our work. Our special thanks to our team at Cengage Learning: Annie Todd, Director of College Success; Laurie Runion, Development Editor; Reynol Junco, "Wired Window" feature; Maggie Barbieri, Editor of "Confessions of a College Student."

At Bedford/St. Martin's, we thank Joan Feinberg, President; Denise Wydra, Editorial Director; Karen Henry, Editor in Chief; Carrie Brandon, Executive Editor; Julie Kelly, Development Editor; Casey Carroll, Marketing Manager; Sarah Guariglia, Editorial Assistant; Nicholas Murphy, Editorial Assistant; Elise Kaiser, Assistant Director of Editing, Design, and Production; and Kerri Cardone, Production Editor.

Most of all, we thank you, the users of our book, for you are the true inspirations for this work.

Step by Step
to College and Career Success

Beginning Your College Experience:

Setting Off on the Right Foot

© John Boykin/PhotoEdit

No matter what your age and background, the fact that you have decided to go to college means you realize how dramatically your college experience can change your life for the better. Yet the sad fact is that many entering students drop out or flunk out. And the highest college dropout rate occurs during the first year of college.

If new students want to succeed, why do some of them make questionable choices? Take the student who left campus before the first day of classes because she was intimidated by the social activities the school had arranged for new students. Or the student who wanted to meet other students so much that he went out every night and never opened a book. Or the one who maxed out his credit card the first week of the term. Or the minority student who felt out of place on a predominantly white campus. Or the returning student who found it was nearly impossible to balance the responsibilities of work, family, and studies. Or those who lacked clear goals for college; couldn't manage their time; or never learned how to study for an exam or use the library, the Internet, and other resources.

This book aims to help you avoid issues such as these. It is a step-by-step guide to experiences and practices geared to college success. Follow these strategies and you can achieve more than you may have dreamed possible in college and your career. ■

In this step you will learn:

- what questions typically are of concern to first-year students
- in what ways college is different from high school
- which issues and circumstances commonly apply to returning students
- what advantages result from a college education
- how to set your own goals for academic success
- how best to connect with your instructors
- why following your campus's guidelines for academic honesty is crucial
- how to create a budget and manage your finances
- what your responsibilities are regarding financial aid

How Do You Measure Up?

Beginning Your College Experience

Check the following items that apply to you:

____ 1. I recognize that many of my worries about starting college are normal.

____ 2. I understand the career and life benefits of a college education.

____ 3. I know how to set short-term goals for my academic success.

____ 4. I plan to get to know my instructors.

____ 5. I understand the importance of participating in class discussions.

____ 6. I welcome constructive criticism about my work.

____ 7. I understand my school's policies with respect to academic honesty.

____ 8. I understand what constitutes plagiarism and cheating.

____ 9. I maintain a budget.

____ 10. I avoid debt so that I don't run out of money.

Review the items you did not check. Paying attention to all these aspects of your college experience can be very important to your success. After reading this Step, come back to this list and choose an item or two that you did not check but are willing to work on.

College
Time
Think
Learn
Clearly
Engage
Read
Test
Relate
Health
Community
Choices

Making a Commitment and Staying Focused

Why do so many students drop out of college in the first year? For those fresh out of high school, a major problem is newfound freedom. Your college instructors are not going to tell you what, how, or when to study. If you live on campus, your parents aren't there to wake you in the morning, see that you eat well and get enough sleep, monitor whether or how carefully you do your homework, and remind you to allow enough time to get to school. Getting it done now depends on you.

For returning students, the opposite is true: Most experience an overwhelming lack of freedom. Working, caring for a family, and meeting other commitments and responsibilities compete for the time and attention it takes to do their best or even simply to persist in college.

Whichever problem you face, what will motivate you to stay focused? And what about the enormous investment of time and money that getting a college degree requires? Are you convinced that the investment will pay off? Or are you having thoughts such as these:

- Will I be able to handle all this freedom? Or will I just waste time?
- I don't know anybody. How am I going to make friends? How can I get involved in campus activities? Whom do I turn to for help when I need it?
- Can I get through college and still manage to take care of my family? What will my family think about all the time I'll have to spend in classes and studying?
- As a minority student, will I be in for some unpleasant surprises?
- Is college going to be too difficult for me? Professors are so much more demanding than high school teachers.
- I hope I won't disappoint the people I care about and who expect so much of me.
- Up to now I've gotten by without working too hard. Now I'll really have to study. Will I be tempted to cut corners or maybe even cheat?
- What if I don't pick the right major? What if I don't know which major is right for me?
- Can I afford college? Can my parents afford it? I wouldn't want them to spend this much and then have me fail.

- Maybe I'm the only one who's feeling like this. Maybe everyone else is just smarter than I am.
- Looking around class makes me feel so old! Will I be able to keep up at my age?
- Will some instructors be biased against students like me?

How College Is Different

The differences between high school and college can also make starting college difficult. Here are some things to expect:

- Depending on where you went to high school, you may be part of a more diverse student body in college.
- You may not feel as unique or special as you might have before, especially if you attend a large university.
- Managing your time will be more complex because classes meet on various days and you may have to juggle commitments such as work, family, activities, and sports.
- There will be more opportunities to make friends—but because many people will be new to you, you'll have to carefully choose those with whom you want to build a lasting relationship.
- Your college classes may have many more students in them and meet for longer periods than classes you've encountered before.
- College tests are given less frequently.
- You will probably do more writing in college.
- Your instructors will rarely have discussions with you about your progress.
- You'll be on your own.
- You will choose from many more types of courses.
- While peer pressure keeps many high school students from interacting with faculty, in college it's the norm to ask a professor for advice or guidance.
- You and your instructors will have more freedom to express different views.
- College instructors usually have private offices and keep regular office hours.
- High school courses tend to be textbook focused, whereas college courses are more lecture focused.
- Some of your courses will require you to do original research.

Many students face the special challenges of balancing the responsibilities of work and school.

© David Young Wolff/PhotoEdit

- College students often have more work to do, both in and out of class.
- Many college students live far from home.

Returning Students versus Traditional Students

Similarly, returning students must deal with major life changes when they begin college:

- Those whose grown children have moved away may find college a liberating experience, a new beginning, a stimulating challenge, or a path to a career.
- Working full-time and attending college at night or on weekends can produce added stress, especially for students with a family at home.
- Returning students tend to work harder than many younger students. Consequently, they also tend to earn higher grades, even though many of them believe they won't be able to keep up with younger classmates.
- Returning students, generally speaking, take their studies more seriously than younger students.
- Age brings with it a wealth of wisdom and experience that, properly used, can help returning students achieve, and even exceed, their goals.

Setting Goals for Success

What can you do to achieve success? One method is to set specific goals as you start your courses that will help you reach your potential.

College is an ideal time to begin setting and fulfilling short- and long-term goals. A short-term goal might be to read twenty pages from your history text twice a week, anticipating an exam that will cover the first hundred pages of the book. A long-term goal

might be to begin predicting which college courses will help you attain your career goals. (It's okay if you don't know which career to pursue; more than 60 percent of college students change majors at least once.)

Start by following these guidelines to set some short-term goals:

1. State your goal in measurable terms. Be specific about what you want to achieve and when.

2. Be sure that the goal is achievable. Allow enough time to pursue it. If you don't have the necessary skills, strengths, and resources to achieve your goal, modify it appropriately.

3. Be sure you genuinely want to achieve the goal. Don't set out to work toward something only because you want to please others.

4. Know why the goal matters. Be sure your goal fits into a larger plan and has the potential to give you a sense of accomplishment.

5. Identify difficulties you might encounter. Plan for ways you might overcome obstacles.

6. Decide which goal comes next. How will you begin? Create steps and a timeline for reaching your next goal.

Advantages of a College Education

According to the Carnegie Commission on Higher Education, these are some of the benefits enjoyed by college graduates:

- You will have a less erratic job history.
- You will earn more promotions.
- You will likely be happier with your work.
- You will be less likely than a nongraduate to become unemployed.
- You not only will earn more with a college degree, you also will find it easier to get a job and hold onto it.

Of course, college will affect you in other ways. A well-rounded college education will expand life's possibilities for you by steeping you in the richness of how the world, the nation, society, and the people around you came to be. As a result:

- You will learn how to work independently and discover new knowledge.
- You will encounter and learn more about how to appreciate the cultural, artistic, and spiritual dimensions of life.
- You will learn more about how to seek appropriate information before making a decision.
- You will grow intellectually through learning about and interacting with cultures, languages, ethnic groups, religions, nationalities, and socioeconomic groups other than your own.

Connecting with **Your Instructors** and **Finding** a Mentor

For some instructors, it's probably much easier to write and deliver a lecture than to engage students in a discussion. But often professors who favor class discussions do so because they believe it's a better way to learn and because it's exciting for them to hear students demonstrate how much they've learned.

Some instructors go the extra mile to make classes interesting, and so should you. Instead of passively blending in with your peers, ask questions in class that other students probably want to ask but don't. Try to do something innovative in each paper and project. You may make some mistakes, but your instructor probably will appreciate your inventiveness, reward you for it, and willingly help you improve your work.

Instructors will set deadlines for work and stick to them. Having to meet firm deadlines should help you see the crucial importance of managing your time. Being late with just one thing can sometimes make the whole plan fall apart. If you're ever unsure about a deadline, ask your professor.

Just as good professors invite you to speak out in class, they also keep the lines of communication open. They not only grade your work but also may ask you how you're learning, what you're learning, and how well you believe they are teaching. In fact, some of the best learning may take place one-on-one in the instructor's office. Your professors will encourage you to develop new ways of thinking, to realize that there may

Resolve to participate in class discussions. Speaking up can play a key role in your college success.

be many acceptable answers as opposed to just one, to challenge existing knowledge, to ask questions in class, and to propose possible solutions to problems. Most colleges and universities guarantee their professors "academic freedom"— the right to study and discuss controversial issues without risk of losing their jobs. In the spirit of academic freedom, professors will invite you to disagree with things they say. But as you make comments or contribute to class discussion, it's important to treat other students and your professor with respect, even when you disagree with them.

You may be surprised to find that most professors do not fit the stereotype of the ivory tower scholar. Although many must spend part of their time doing research, a majority of them report that their favorite activity is teaching. Most instructors also want to get to know their students. They appreciate your taking advantage of office hours, study sessions, and other opportunities for one-to-one interaction. The relationships that you develop with your instructors will be to your advantage when you need extra help or that all important reference letter. And research shows that students who stay in touch with their instructors out of class have a greater chance of doing well in college.

Finding a Mentor

A mentor is a person who is now, in some respects, what you hope to be in the future. What mentors have you had? What specific qualities have you tried to emulate? What might you be seeking in a college mentor?

If you don't have a mentor, how might you find one during your first year of college? Look for the person who takes a special interest in you, who encourages you to challenge yourself, who willingly listens to you when you have questions or problems, and who offers to meet with you to discuss your work. A mentor may be an academic adviser, an instructor, the chairperson of a department, an older student, or anyone else who is willing to offer interest, wisdom, and support. Most importantly, find a person whom you can trust and who is genuinely interested in your well-being but asks little or nothing in return.

Making the Most of Relationships with Your Instructors

Attend class regularly and be on time. Learning what your instructors have to offer is much easier when you're there every day.

Participate in class. Seek instructors who favor active student engagement in learning; you'll find learning is more fun this way, you'll learn more, and you'll earn higher grades.

Learn from your instructors' criticism. Criticism can be healthy and helpful. It's how we all learn. If you get a low grade, ask to meet with your instructor to discuss what you should do to improve your work.

Meet with your instructors. You should make it a point to meet with instructors if you have something to discuss. Students who do so tend to do better academically. Your instructors are required to have office hours; they expect you to visit.

Practicing Academic Honesty

Colleges and universities have academic integrity policies or honor codes that clearly define cheating, lying, plagiarism, and other forms of dishonest conduct. Integrity is a cornerstone of higher education, and actions that compromise integrity can damage everyone: you, your classmates, your college or university, your community, and ultimately the country.

It is often difficult to know how campus rules about dishonest conduct apply to specific situations. The following information will help you sort out and understand the issues.

Types of Misconduct

Institutions vary widely in how they define broad terms such as lying or cheating. One university defines cheating as "intentionally using or attempting to use unauthorized materials, information, notes, study aids, or other devices . . . [including] unauthorized communication of information during an academic exercise." This would apply to looking over a classmate's shoulder for an answer, using a calculator when it is not authorized, procuring or discussing an exam (or individual questions from an exam) without permission, copying lab notes that you will turn in for a grade, purchasing term papers over the Internet, and watching the video or movie instead of reading the book.

Plagiarism, taking another person's ideas or work and presenting them as your own, is especially intolerable in academic culture. Just as taking someone else's property constitutes physical theft, taking credit for someone else's ideas constitutes intellectual theft.

On most tests, you do not have to credit specific individuals. (But some instructors do require such acknowledgments; when in doubt, ask.) In written reports and papers, however, you must give credit any time you use any of the following:

- Another person's actual words
- Another person's ideas or theories—even if you don't quote them directly
- Any other information not considered common knowledge

Many colleges and universities prohibit other, and more specific, forms of dishonesty. Examples of prohibited behaviors include intentionally inventing information or results, earning credit more than once for the same piece of academic work without permission, giving your work or exam answers to another student to copy during the actual exam or before the exam is given to another section, and bribing in exchange for any kind of academic advantage. Most schools also outlaw helping or attempting to help another student commit a dishonest act.

How Cheating Hurts Everyone

You may think that cheating is harmless, but in reality it has far-reaching effects. If you cheat, however you accomplish it, you are doing something that is ethically wrong and unfair to yourself and to other students, that shortchanges your ability to learn, and that may result in serious penalties, including course failure and even expulsion from school. And cheating can easily become a habit, one that will likely catch up

© Digital Vision/Getty Images

When all is said and done, cheating hurts everyone.

with you at some critical point in your life. As a college student, it's crucial that you trust your ability to learn and that you devote the time and energy necessary to do your own work.

Reasons for Misconduct

To avoid becoming intentionally or unintentionally involved in academic misconduct, consider the reasons it could happen:

Ignorance In a survey at the University of South Carolina, 20 percent of students incorrectly thought that buying a term paper wasn't cheating. Forty percent thought using a test file (a collection of actual tests from previous terms) was fair behavior. Sixty percent thought it was all right to get answers from someone who had taken an exam earlier in the same term or in a prior term. What do you think?

Cultural and campus differences In other countries and on some U.S. campuses, students are encouraged to review past exams as practice exercises. Some student groups or associations maintain test files for use by students. Some campuses permit sharing answers and information for homework and other assignments with friends.

Different policies among instructors Because there is no universal code that dictates such behaviors, ask your instructors for clarification. When a student is caught violating the academic code of a particular college or instructor, pleading ignorance of the rules is a weak defense.

A belief that grades—not learning— are everything Actually the reverse is true. This mistaken thinking may reflect our society's competitive atmosphere. It also may be the result of pressure from

parents, peers, or professors. In truth, grades are nothing if one has cheated to earn them.

Lack of preparation or inability to manage time and activities If you think you don't have enough time to do your own work on an assignment, before you consider cheating, ask an instructor to extend the deadline.

STRATEGIES

Ensuring Academic Honesty

Here are some steps you can take to reduce the likelihood of problems:

1. Know the rules. Learn the academic code for your college or university. Study the requirements on course syllabi. If an instructor does not clarify standards and expectations, ask exactly what they are.
2. Set clear boundaries. Refuse to "help" others who ask you to help them cheat. Resisting their pressure may be hard to do, but you've got to say no. In test settings, keep your answers covered and your eyes down, and put all extraneous materials away, including cell phones. Now that many cell phones enable text messaging, instructors are rightfully suspicious when they see students using their cell phones during an exam.
3. Improve time management. Be well prepared for all quizzes, exams, projects, and papers. This may mean unlearning habits such as procrastination (see the Step on time management and motivation for more information).
4. Seek help. Find out where you can obtain assistance with study skills, time management, and test taking. If your methods are sound but the content of the course is too difficult, see your instructor, join a study group, or visit your campus learning center or tutorial service.
5. Withdraw from the course. Your college has a policy about dropping courses and a last day to drop without penalty. You may decide only to drop the course that's giving you trouble. But you may choose to withdraw from all classes and take time off before returning if you find yourself in over your head or if a long illness, a family crisis, or some other unexpected occurrence has caused you to fall behind. Before you withdraw, you should ask about campus policies, as well as about the possible effects of withdrawing on federal financial aid and other scholarship programs. Talk to your adviser or counselor.
6. Re-examine goals. Stick to your own realistic goals instead of giving in to pressure from family or friends to achieve impossibly high standards. You may also feel pressure to enter a particular career or profession of little or no interest to you. If so, sit down with counseling or career professionals or your academic adviser and explore alternatives.

Managing Your Finances and Controlling Your Debt

If you're like most college students, your income will be limited, but you'll suddenly have more reasons to spend. First-year students generally have some assumptions about the quality of life they want in college. That may be one reason why accepting a change in lifestyle to accommodate college costs is so difficult for many of them. Even though you're almost certain to be confronted with unexpected expenses and money shortages, you can learn to handle these new responsibilities by understanding how to create a budget and manage your finances.

Developing a Budget

Before you can develop a budget, you will need to track and begin to understand your spending habits. In college, you'll have many expenses that recur at regular intervals, such as tuition, books, and room and board. Other expenses do not occur regularly and thus are difficult to track—for example, the costs of entertainment and clothes. It's easy to say at the end of the month, "I have no idea where all my money went." That's why it's important to create a system for tracking your expenses, so you can plan for major events such as spring break and study abroad. And because a budget is only as good as the person who keeps it, you not only need to work hard to develop an accurate and honest budgeting method but you also need to stick to it.

To get started, let's focus on two types of expenses: fixed and monthly. Fixed expenses are predetermined, recurring expenses such as rent and tuition. These expenses are often large and require planning (withdrawing money from a savings account or taking out a loan). Monthly expenses tend to be smaller and vary from month to month; they include costs such as phone charges and entertainment.

If you find it hard to begin making a budget, try this approach. For one week, keep track of how much you spend and what you spend it on. Then take that list and place each expense into a category, such as entertainment, clothes, transportation, and so forth. Now multiply by four to get your anticipated monthly expenses. This estimate will help you get started, but you will want to refine your system until it's as accurate as possible.

Now that you have begun the monthly challenge of living on a budget, remember to plan ahead for non-recurring expenses such as birthday and Christmas gifts. Consider your budget a working document that is reviewed monthly. It will probably take several months to develop an effective plan, but after that your budget will become part of your lifestyle. Following your budget not only will help you reduce stress but also, if you stick with it, can serve you well in many ways throughout your college years.

Treating Credit and Debit Cards Wisely

Credit card companies have increased their marketing to college students significantly over the past decade so that almost all college students have a credit or debit card and many have multiple cards. Credit card companies wow you with fantastic deals. Retail chain stores offer their own cards and entice potential cardholders with 10 percent or more off their next purchase. It can be difficult to make decisions about credit cards when you are just beginning to learn how to manage your money and at the same time are establishing a credit history.

Many people view using a credit card as an easy way to establish a positive credit history. But if you

© David Butow/Corbis SABA

don't use the card wisely, you may owe more than you can afford to pay, damage your credit rating, and create credit problems that are difficult to fix. A positive credit history is an asset when you are applying for a loan or even a job. It is important to understand how decisions early in your credit history will affect your future. Credit cards, when used responsibly, benefit the holder in many ways, but they can also be real trouble. A good rule of thumb is to have no more credit available to you than you can pay off in two months.

By using a debit card rather than credit cards, you will restrict your spending to the amount of money in your bank account. However, since debit cards provide access to your bank account, you should keep your card in a safe place, away from a personal identification number (PIN). The safest way to protect your account is to memorize your PIN. If you're afraid you'll forget it, write it down and put it in a secure location. Do not use a PIN that is the number of your street address, your birth date, your phone number, or other numbers tied to you personally. People who know you may be able to guess the number. Bank studies show that about one-third of ATM fraud occurs because the cardholder wrote the PIN on the card or on slips of paper with the card.

Staying Out of Financial Trouble

Many students have problems with finances during college. It's important to be committed to preventing and resolving those problems.

Protect your personal and financial information

Credit or debit cards and their numbers, your social security number, your bank statement, and your checkbook are items that can be stolen and used by other people. Be sure to keep them in a safe place out of public view. While some people may want only your money, others might be trying to steal your identity. By using your social security number, address, and bank account, identity thieves may rent an apartment, obtain a credit card, borrow money, or establish a telephone account in your name. A simple way to help protect your credit card is to write the words "picture ID required" under your signature on the credit card. When a clerk checks the signature, she or he should ask for a photo ID. Another way to protect yourself is to join a credit card registry. For a small fee, this service automatically notifies all of your credit card companies when you lose a card, and requests replacements.

Deal with creditors sooner rather than later
Don't put financial problems on the back burner. Debt will only get larger if you don't deal with it head on. As soon as you begin to experience difficulties, contact your creditors. Most creditors will help you develop a reasonable repayment plan. Don't wait until your creditors have turned your account over to a collection agency.

If you don't know what else to do, talk with someone you trust who understands your financial problems. Parents and relatives can be sources of good advice, or financial counselors may be available to you on campus. Your financial aid office may be able to point you toward reputable people who can assist you.

Holding Down Your College Debt

Financial aid to help you pay for college comes from many sources. Most of this aid is awarded to students on the basis of a demonstrated financial need and/or recognition of some identifiable talent (such as top grades for an academic scholarship).

Remember that although the financial aid office is there to serve you, you must become your own advocate. The following tips should help:

- File for financial aid every year. Even if you don't think you will receive aid in a certain year, you must file yearly in case you become eligible in the future.
- Meet all filing deadline dates. Financial aid is awarded from fixed funds. When the money has been awarded, there is usually none left for late applicants. Students who do not meet filing deadlines risk losing aid from one year to the next.
- Talk with your financial aid officer immediately if you or your family experiences a significant loss (loss of a job or death of a parent or spouse).
- Inquire every year about criteria-based aid. Many colleges and universities have grants and scholarships for students who meet specific criteria. These may include grants for minority students, students in specific academic majors, and students of single parents.
- Inquire about campus jobs throughout the year. If you do not have a job and want or need to work, keep asking about jobs, as they can open up at any time. Be aware that students who work on campus have a higher probability of graduating than students who work off campus.
- Consider requesting a reassessment. If you have reviewed your financial aid package and think that your circumstances deserve additional consideration, you can ask the financial aid office to reassess your eligibility. The office is not always required to do so, but the request may be worth your effort.

Where to Go for Help: On Campus

To find the college support services you need, ask your academic adviser or counselor; consult your college catalog, phone book, and home page on the Internet. Or call or visit student services (or student affairs).

Academic advisement center: Help in choosing courses, information on degree requirements.

Academic skills center: Tutoring, help in study and memory skills, help in studying for exams.

Adult re-entry center: Programs for returning students, supportive contacts with other adult students, information about services such as child care.

Career center: Career library, interest assessments, counseling, help in finding a major, job and internship listings.

Commuter services: List of off-campus housing, roommate lists, orientation to community.

Computer center: Minicourses, handouts on campus computer resources.

Counseling center: Confidential counseling on personal concerns. Stress management programs.

Disabled student services: Assistance in overcoming physical barriers and learning disabilities.

Financial Aid and Scholarship Office: Information on financial aid programs, scholarships, and grants.

Health center: Help with personal nutrition, weight control, exercise, and issues related to sexuality.

Housing office: Help in locating on- or off-campus housing.

Math center: Help with math skills.

Writing center: Help with writing assignments.

WIRED WINDOW

THE INTERNET OFFERS a number of ways to get connected online. As you might already know, social networking websites like Facebook and MySpace are a great way to connect to your friends. Is Facebook popular at your college? If so, take advantage of its networking potential. Through Facebook, you can find new schoolmates with similar interests, join clubs or interest groups, and find friends in your classes. Keep in mind that information that you post on Facebook is available to everyone in your network unless you adjust your privacy settings. While most students use Facebook and MySpace appropriately, some students have faced institutional (and sometimes legal) sanctions for pictures and information they posted online. Therefore, it is important that you review your profile to make sure that you are only including information you want the public to know about you.

Another way you can learn about your specific college is by taking advantage of official and unofficial online campus resources. Your institution's website is one official resource that you might find useful for discovering a range of information, from how to get help with your writing to when the semester break begins. Unofficial resources include websites that rate professors and student-run wikis that help you find answers to common questions about your college or university. A popular website for rating professors is at http://www.RateMyProfessor.com. Keep in mind that ratings on these websites were not reviewed for accuracy, so use them only as a starting point to learn about your professor.

▶▶▶ BUILDING YOUR PORTFOLIO

Credit Cards...A Slippery Slope!

Life was a lot simpler when what we honored was father
and mother rather than all major credit cards.

-Robert Orben (b. 1927), U.S. magician and comedy writer

Remember the saying "there is no free lunch"? That is a good maxim to keep in mind as you consider adding credit cards to your financial picture. Credit card companies often target college students with offers for a free T-shirt or discounts if they sign up for a new card. While it might seem harmless at the time, signing up for multiple credit cards can get you in financial trouble...
and fast!

Let's take a look at one credit card offer available to college students and see just what the fine print has to say. Google "Student Visa Credit Card." You'll find many such cards offered. Pick one for your review.

1. Read all about it

   View the terms, conditions, and fees associated with a student Visa credit card offered to college students.

2. What does it all mean?

   a. What is the Annual Percentage Rate (APR) for purchases using this card?
   APR: _____%

   b. What is the APR or Transaction Fee for a bank or ATM cash advance using this card?
   Cash Advance: _____

   c. How long is the grace period for this card (the number of days between the statement closing date and the payment due date)?
   Grace Period: _____

   d. What would happen to the APR if you made a late payment, went over your credit limit, or made a payment that was not honored on this card?

   _____

Quick Reference

A big factor in effectively managing your credit card debt is being aware of the terms and fees that apply to each account you have. If you have credit cards (including gas cards and store credit cards such as a Gap or Sears credit card), find your last billing statement and make yourself a quick reference guide in your portfolio. Create a new entry in your portfolio for this activity with the title Quick Reference. Record your work for this assignment there.

Managing Time and Staying Motivated:

The Starting Line for Academic Success

© Gary Gerovac/Masterfile

How do you finish everything in your day?

How do you approach time? Because people have different personalities and come from different cultures, you and others may view time in different ways.

The way you look at time may also have to do with your preferred style of learning. For example, if you're a natural organizer, you probably enter on your calendar or handheld personal digital assistant (PDA) all due dates for assignments, exams, and quizzes as soon as you receive each course syllabus, and you may be good at adhering to a strict schedule. On the other hand, if you take a laid-back approach to life, you may prefer to be more flexible, or "go with the flow," rather than follow a daily or weekly schedule. You may excel at dealing with the unexpected, but you may also be a procrastinator.

Time management involves six components: knowing your goals, setting priorities to meet them, anticipating the unexpected, placing yourself in control of your time, making a commitment to being punctual, and carrying out your plans. This Step addresses essential strategies to help you manage your time. Being a good time manager is one of the key skills of successful college students and a quality that every employer seeks. ■

- how to take control of your time and your life

- how to use goals and objectives to guide your planning

- how to prioritize your use of time

- how to combat procrastination and maintain motivation

- how to use a daily planner and other tools

- how to organize your day, your week, and your academic term

- what value a "to-do" list provides

- how to avoid overextending yourself and giving in to distractions

- how time management relates to courtesy and respect in the classroom and on campus

How Do You Measure Up?

Managing Time and Staying Motivated

Check the following items that apply to you:

_____ 1. It is important for me to feel I am in control of my time.

_____ 2. I understand how my background (family, culture, lifestyle, commitments, gender, age, and other factors) influences my approach to time management.

_____ 3. I set academic and personal goals every term to guide how I prioritize my time.

_____ 4. I am able to focus on the task at hand instead of getting distracted or procrastinating.

_____ 5. I know my most productive times of the day.

_____ 6. I use a daily or weekly planner or some other type of planning device (a PDA, for example) to keep track of my commitments.

_____ 7. I maintain a "to-do" list to keep track of the tasks I must complete.

_____ 8. I am able to balance my social life and my need for personal time with my academic requirements.

_____ 9. I am able to say "no" to requests so that I do not become overextended.

_____ 10. I am punctual and almost never turn in an assignment late, skip class, or miss an appointment.

Review the items you did not check. Paying attention to all these aspects of your college experience can be very important to your success. After reading this Step, come back to this list and choose an item or two that you did not check but are willing to work on.

Jeanne L. Higbee of the University of Minnesota, Twin Cities and Mary Ellen O'Leary of the University of South Carolina contributed their valuable and considerable expertise to the writing of this section.

Taking Control of Your Time

The first step to effective time management is recognizing that you can be in control. Being in control means that you make your own decisions. Two of the most often-cited differences between high school and college are increased autonomy, or independence, and greater responsibility. If you are a returning student rather than a recent high school graduate, it's likely that you already have considerable independence. But returning to college creates responsibilities above and beyond those you already have, whether they include employment, family, community service, or other activities.

Whether you are beginning college immediately after high school or continuing your education after a hiatus, now is the time to establish new priorities for managing your time. To take control of your life and your time and to guide your decisions, it is wise to begin by setting some goals for the future.

Setting Goals

Where do you see yourself five or ten years from now? What are some of your goals for the coming decade? One goal is probably to earn a two-year or four-year degree or technical certificate. You already may have decided on the career that you want to pursue. Or perhaps you plan to go on to graduate or professional school. As you look to the future, you may see yourself buying a new car, owning a home, starting a family, owning a business, or retiring early. Time management is one of the most effective tools to assist you in meeting such goals.

Take a few minutes to complete the "Try It!" exercise. List your top three personal goals for the coming decade. Your goals can be challenging, but they should also be attainable. Then determine at least two methods for achieving each goal. The difference between a goal and an objective is that a goal is what you want to achieve, while an objective is a tangible, measurable method for getting there.

More than likely, one goal you will set is to find a good job upon completion of your degree, or a job that is significantly better than your current job. Your objectives may include defining a "good job," making yourself a competitive candidate in a job search, and completing an internship in a related field, among others.

In a job search, a college degree and good grades may not be enough. So when setting goals and objectives for allocating your time, consider the importance of having a well-rounded résumé when you graduate.

Such a résumé might show that you made a commitment to participating in extracurricular activities, gaining leadership experience, engaging in community service or in an internship or co-op opportunities, developing job-related skills, keeping up-to-date on technological advances, or pursuing relevant part- or full-time employment while attending classes.

When it is time to look for a permanent job, you want to demonstrate that you have used your college years wisely. Doing so will require planning and effective time-management skills that employers value very highly. Your college or university's career center can help you arrange for an internship, a co-op, or opportunities for community service that will give you valuable experience and strengthen your résumé.

Establishing Priorities

Once you have established goals and objectives, prioritize your time. Which goals and objectives are the most important to you? For example, is it more important to study for a test tomorrow or to attend a job fair today? That will be up to you. Keep in mind that it isn't always a good idea to ignore long-term goals in order to meet short-term goals. Using good time management, you can study during the week before the test so that you can attend the job fair the day before the test. One way that skilled time managers establish priorities is to

TRY IT! Goal Setting

A. Name your top three goals for the coming decade.

1. _____
2. _____
3. _____

B. List two measurable objectives for achieving each of the goals set above.

1. a. _____
   b. _____
2. a. _____
   b. _____
3. a. _____
   b. _____

maintain a "to-do" list (discussed in more detail later in this step), to rank the items on the list, and then determine schedules and deadlines for each task.

Another aspect of setting priorities in college is finding an appropriate way to balance an academic schedule, social life, and time alone. All work and no play can make you dull or uninteresting and can also undermine your academic motivation. Similarly, never having time alone or time to study and think can leave you feeling out of control. For many students the greatest challenge of prioritizing is to balance college with work and family obligations that are equally important and not "optional." But social activities are also an important part of the college experience, and being involved in campus life enhances student satisfaction, achievement, and retention.

Staying Focused

Many of the decisions you make today are reversible. You may change your major, and your career and life goals may shift as well. But the decision to take control of your life—to establish your own goals for the future, to set your priorities, and to manage your time accordingly—is an important one.

If you are an adult re-entering college, you may question your decision to go back to school, and you

Some college students have to juggle taking care of children and pursuing a degree.

may feel temporarily overwhelmed by the academic responsibilities that are suddenly heaped on top of your other commitments. Prioritizing, rethinking some commitments, letting some things go, and weighing the advantages and disadvantages of attending college part time versus full time can help you work through this adjustment eriod. Again, keep your long-term goals in mind.

Successful people frequently say that staying focused is a key to their success. To help you stay focused, make a plan. Begin with your priorities, and then think about the necessities of life.

Finish what needs to be done before you move from work to pleasure.

Overcoming Procrastination and Staying Motivated

Procrastination can trip up many otherwise capable people. Students may procrastinate for a number of reasons. Some procrastinate because they are perfectionists; not doing a task may be easier than having to live up to their own or others' expectations. Others procrastinate because they find an assigned task boring or irrelevant. But simply not enjoying an assignment is not a good excuse to put it off. We all have to do things we consider boring, distasteful, or irrelevant but, unfortunately, we don't have the option of ignoring them.

Regardless of its source, procrastination may be your single greatest enemy. Here are some ways to beat procrastination and to stay motivated:

- Tell yourself, "I need to do this now, and I am going to do this now." Remind yourself of the possible consequences if you do not get down to work.
- Create a "to-do" list. Check off things as you finish them. Use the list to focus on tasks that aren't getting done. Move them to the top of your next day's list, and make up your mind to do them.
- Break down big jobs into smaller steps. Tackle short, easy-to-accomplish tasks first.
- Before you begin to work, promise yourself a reward for finishing the task.
- Control your study environment. Eliminate distractions. Say "no" to friends and family who want your attention.
- Don't make or take phone calls or send or receive email during planned study sessions. Close your door.

If these ideas fail to motivate you, re-examine your values and priorities. What is really important to you? If you are not willing to tackle the tasks at hand, you may want to reconsider whether you should be in college at this time.

Creating a Workable Class Schedule

If you are a first-year student, you may not have had much flexibility in determining your course schedule; by the time you could register for classes, some sections of your required courses already may have been closed. You also may not have known whether you would prefer taking classes back-to-back or having a break between classes.

Over time, have you found that you prefer spreading your classes over five or six days of the week? Or have you discovered that you like to go to class just two or three days a week, or only once a week for a longer class period? Your attention span as well as your other commitments may influence your decisions about your class schedule. Before you register for the next term, think about how to make your class schedule work for you—how you can create a schedule that allows you to use your time most efficiently and effectively.

Using a Daily or Weekly Planner

In college, as in life, you will quickly learn that managing time is an important key not only to survival but also to success. A good way to start is to look at the big picture. Consider buying a week-at-a-glance organizer for the current year. Your campus bookstore may sell one designed just for your college or university, with important dates and deadlines already provided. If you prefer to use an electronic planner, that's fine—your PC, laptop, or PDA comes equipped with a calendar.

Regardless of the format you prefer (electronic or on paper), carry your planner with you at all times and continue to enter all due dates as soon as you know them. Write in meeting times and locations, scheduled social events, study time for each class, and so forth. Jot down phone numbers and email addresses, too, in case something comes up and you need to cancel. Get

into the habit of using a planner to help you keep track of commitments and maintain control of your schedule. This practice will become invaluable to you in the world of work. Choose a specific time of day to check your notes daily for the current week and the coming week. It takes just a moment to be certain that you aren't forgetting something important, and it helps relieve stress!

Maintaining a "To-Do" List

Keeping a "to-do" list can also help you avoid feeling stressed or out of control. Some people start a new list every day or once a week. Others keep a running list and only throw a page away when everything on the list is done. Use your "to-do" list to keep track of all the tasks you need to remember, not just academics. You might

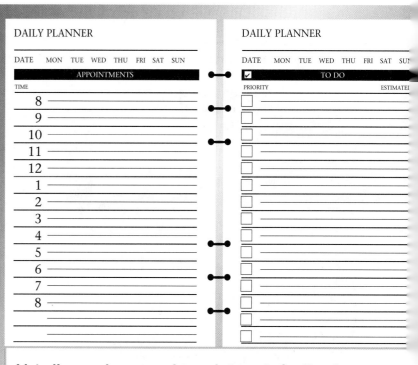

List all your classes and appointments for the day on the left page. Enter your "to-do" list for the day on the right page. In the boxes, indicate A for top priority, B for a lower priority, and so on. Then return to the left page to schedule times to complete your highest-priority tasks.

include errands you need to run, appointments you must make, email messages you need to send, and so on.

Develop a system for prioritizing the items on your list: highlight; use colored ink; or mark with one, two, or three stars or A, B, C. You can use your "to-do" list in conjunction with your planner. As you complete each task, cross it off. You will feel good about how much you have accomplished, and this positive feeling will help you to stay motivated.

Scheduling Your Time Week by Week

Use the following steps to schedule your time for a whole week at a time:

- Begin by entering all of your commitments for the week—classes, work hours, family commitments, and so on—on your schedule.
- Try to reserve at least two hours of study time for each hour spent in class. This two-for-one rule reflects many faculty members' expectations for how much work you should do to master the material in their classes. This rule says that if you are taking a typical full-time class load of fifteen credits, for example, you should plan to study an additional thirty hours per week. Think of this forty-five-hour-per-week commitment as comparable to a full-time job. Then if you are also working, reconsider how many hours per week it will be reasonable for you to be employed above and beyond this commitment, or consider reducing your credit load. At many institutions you need to carry a minimum of twelve or thirteen credits to be considered a full-time student, and this status can be important for financial aid and various forms of insurance.
- Depending on your body clock, obligations, and potential distractions, decide whether you will study more effectively in the day or in the evening or by using a combination of both. Determine whether you are capable of getting up very early in the morning to study, or how late you can stay up at night and still wake up for morning classes.
- Estimate how much time you will need for each assignment, and plan to begin your work early. A good time manager frequently finishes assignments before actual due dates to allow for emergencies.
- Set aside time for research and other preparatory tasks. For example, instructors may expect you to be computer literate, but they usually don't have time to explain how to use a word processor, spreadsheet, or statistical computer program. Most campuses have learning centers or computer centers that offer tutoring, walk-in assistance, or workshops to assist you with computer programs, email, and Internet

TRY IT!

Working Together: Comparing Class Schedules

In a small group, share your current class schedules with the other students. Exchange ideas on how to handle time management problems and the challenges you see in others' schedules. Discuss how you would arrange your schedule differently for the next term.

Time

searches. Your library may offer sessions on searching for information using various computer databases. Such services will save you time and usually are free.

- Schedule at least three aerobic workouts per week. (Walking to and from classes doesn't count.) Taking a break for physical activity relaxes your body, clears your mind, and is a powerful motivator. Choose from brisk walking, running, biking, skating, and a wide variety of team sports, such as volleyball and tennis. Allow enough time to maintain an elevated heart rate for thirty minutes, plus time for warming up, stretching, and cooling down.

© Imagestate Royalty Free/Alamy

Aerobic exercise promotes relaxation and clear thinking and is a powerful motivator.

Organizing Your Day

Being a good student does not necessarily mean studying day and night and doing little else. Keep the following points in mind as you organize your day:

- Set realistic goals for your study time. Assess how long it takes to read a chapter in different types of textbooks and how long you require to review your notes from different instructors, and then schedule your time accordingly. Allow adequate time to review and then test your knowledge when preparing for exams.
- Use waiting time (on the bus, before class, waiting for appointments) to review.
- Schedule time to review as soon as possible after class; you'll remember more of what you learned in class. (You may be able to review right after class if you are not too burned out to concentrate.)
- Take advantage of your best times of day to study. Schedule other activities, such as doing laundry, responding to email, and spending time with friends for times when it will be difficult to concentrate.
- Schedule time right before and after meals for leisure activities; it's hard to study on an empty or a full stomach.
- Use the same study area regularly. Have everything handy that you may need, such as a dictionary, writing implements, a highlighter, and note cards. Make sure that you have adequate lighting, a chair with sufficient back support, and enough desk space to spread out everything you need. When working at a computer, position the keyboard at an appropriate height and adjust monitor settings to avoid eye strain.
- Assess your attention level. Make sure that you are studying actively and that you can meaningfully put what you have learned into words.
- Study difficult or boring subjects first, when you are fresh. (Exception: If you are having trouble getting started, it might be easier to begin with your favorite subject.)
- Divide study time into fifty-minute blocks. Study for fifty minutes; then take a ten- or fifteen-minute break; then study for another fifty-minute block. Try not to study for more than three fifty-minute blocks in a row, or you will find that you are not accomplishing fifty minutes' worth of work. (In economics, this is known as the "law of diminishing returns.")

- Break extended study sessions into a variety of activities, each with a specific objective. For example, begin by reading, then develop flash cards by writing key terms and their definitions or key formulas on note cards, and finally test yourself on what you have read. You cannot maintain maximum concentration when reading in the same text for three consecutive hours.
- Restrict repetitive, distracting, and time-consuming tasks such as checking your email to a certain time, not every hour.
- Avoid multitasking. Even though you may be good at juggling many tasks at once, or at least think that you are, the reality is that you will study more effectively and retain more if you concentrate on one task at a time.
- Be flexible! You cannot anticipate every disruption to your plans. Build extra time into your study schedule so that unexpected interruptions do not prevent you from meeting your goals.
- Reward yourself! Develop a system of short- and long-term study goals and rewards for meeting those goals. Doing so will keep your motivation high.

Make Your Daily Time Management Plan Work

Consider what kind of schedule will work best for you. If you live on campus, you may want to create a schedule

© David Young Wolff/PhotoEdit

Multitasking while completing class assignments makes for inefficient studying.

that situates you near a dining hall at mealtimes or allows you to spend breaks between classes at the library. Or you may need breaks in your schedule for relaxation, like spending time in a student lounge or at the campus center. You may want to avoid returning to your residence hall room to take a nap between classes if the result might be feeling lethargic or oversleeping and missing later classes. Be realistic about your personal habits when choosing class times and locations. Also, if you attend a large college or university be sure that you allow adequate time to get from building to building.

If you're a commuting student, or if you must work off campus in order to afford going to school, you may prefer scheduling your classes together in blocks without breaks. *Block scheduling*, which means enrolling in back-to-back classes, allows you to cut travel time by attending classes one or two days a week, and it may provide more flexibility for scheduling employment or family commitments. But it also can have significant drawbacks:

- You will have little time to process information or to study between classes.
- If you become ill on a class day, you can fall behind in all of your classes.
- You may become fatigued sitting in class after class.
- It will be impossible to have a last-minute study period immediately before a test because you will be attending another class and are likely to have no more than a fifteen-minute break.
- Many exams may be held on the same day.

Don't Overextend Yourself

Being overextended is a primary source of stress for college students. Determine what a realistic workload is for you. Do not take on more than you can handle. Learn to say "no." Do not feel obligated to provide a reason; you have the right to decline requests that will prevent you from getting your own work done.

With the best intentions, even students who use a time management plan can become over-extended. If there is not enough time to carry your course load and to meet your commitments, drop a course before the drop date so you won't have a low grade on your permanent record.

If dropping a course is not feasible and if other activities are lower on your list of priorities, assess your other time commitments and let go of one or more. Doing so can be difficult, especially if you think that you are letting other people down. However, it is far preferable to excuse yourself from an activity in a way that is respectful to others than to fail to come through at the last minute because you are over-committed.

Reduce Distractions and Follow a Routine

Where is the best place to study? Do not study in places associated with leisure, such as at the kitchen table and the living room in front of the TV, because they lend themselves to interruptions by those around you and to other distractions. Similarly it is unwise to study on your bed. You may find yourself drifting off to sleep when you need to study, or you may learn to associate your bed with studying and not be able to go to sleep when you need to. Instead, find quiet places, both on campus and at home, where you can concentrate and develop a study mind-set each time you sit down to do your work.

Stick to a study routine. The more firmly you have established a specific time and a quiet place to study, the more effective you will be in keeping up with your schedule. If you have larger blocks of time available on the weekend, for example, take advantage of them to review or to catch up on major projects, such as term papers, that you can't complete in fifty-minute blocks. By breaking down large tasks and taking one thing at a time, you will make steady progress toward your academic goals and thereby stay motivated.

Studying

Here are additional tips to help you deal with distraction:

- Don't eat while you study. You want your body and mind to be focused on thinking, not digesting.
- Leave the TV, CD player, DVD player, MP3 player, and radio off unless the background noise or music truly helps you concentrate on your studies or drowns out more distracting noises.
- Don't let personal concerns interfere with studying. If necessary, call a friend or write in a journal before you start to study, and then put your worries away.
- Develop an agreement with the people who live with you about quiet hours.

Time Management and Civility

Civility refers to basic politeness or good manners inside and outside the classroom, as well as to our style of communicating with one another. Civility really is all about extending respect to others. In recent years, college educators have begun to focus much more on this issue because of the widespread belief that levels of fundamental civility have been declining. Many of the types of disrespectful behaviors frequently mentioned by faculty members are in some way related to time management, most notably the practices of repeatedly arriving late for class and leaving before class periods have officially ended. But surfing the web or texting your friends during class also shows a lack of respect for both your instructor and your classmates.

At times what instructors perceive as inappropriate or disrespectful behavior may be the result of a cultural misunderstanding. All cultures view time differently. In American academic culture, punctuality is a virtue. Being strictly on time may be a difficult adjustment for you if you grew up in a culture that is more flexible in its approach to time, but it is important to recognize the values of the new culture you are encountering. Although you should not have to alter your cultural identity in order to succeed in college, you must be aware of the expectations that faculty members typically have for students.

Here are a few basic guidelines for respectful behavior in class and in other interactions with instructors.

- Be in class on time. Arrive early enough to remove outerwear, shuffle through your backpack, and have your assignments, notebooks, and writing tools ready to go.

- Avoid behavior in class that shows a lack of respect for the instructor and other students. Such inconsiderate behavior includes walking out in the middle of class to plug a parking meter; answering your cell phone, text-messaging, or surfing the web; doing homework for another class; falling asleep; and whispering or talking.

- Make adequate transportation plans in advance, get enough sleep at night, wake up early enough to be on time for class, and complete assignments prior to class.

- Manage your time when participating in class discussions and activities. Don't "hog the floor"; give others the opportunity to express their ideas. But do take the time to listen respectfully, to suspend judgment, and to weigh the merits of different arguments before forming and expressing your own opinions and answers.

- Be on time for scheduled appointments with your instructor or adviser. If you fail to show up on time, you cause inconvenience not only to the faculty or staff member but also potentially to other students, who, like you, face constant challenges in managing their time.

Time management is a lifelong skill. The more effectively you manage your own time, the more likely it is that you will have a better job after college and that you may be managing the time of other people whom you supervise. It is critical to understand the importance of demonstrating respect for others through your approach to managing your own time.

rrive at class early. Not only will you ave time to get organized before ass starts but you'll also avoid stracting others.

Where to Go for Help

Here are useful resources for advice on managing your time.

On Campus

Academic skills center: Along with assistance in studying for exams, reading textbooks, and taking notes, your campus academic skills center has specialists in time management who can offer advice for your specific problems.

Counseling center: This is a source to consider if your challenges with time management involve personal problems you are unable to resolve.

Your academic adviser/counselor: Your academic advisor or counselor may be able to offer advice or to refer you to a specialist on campus, including someone in one of the offices mentioned previously.

A fellow student: A friend and good student who is willing to help you with time management can be one of your most valuable resources.

Online

Dartmouth College Academic Skills Center:
http://www.dartmouth.edu/~acskills/success/time.html
This website offers tips and resources for managing your time. Under "Time Management Resources," click to view the Time Management Video.

WIRED WINDOW

THE TECHNOLOGY WE use daily is a catch-22. On the one hand, technology helps us to be more productive and organize our time efficiently. On the other hand, technology becomes a colossal distraction and a time-waster. College students spend a lot of time chatting online by using instant messaging software. Think about how you use instant messaging. How often do you use it while doing something else on the computer? Generally, this kind of multitasking is harmless and often helpful when you are trying to do your "digital errands" like paying bills, buying books, and so on. However, because it is so easy to multitask, many students also try to do their school work while surfing the web or IM'ing. Have you ever completed your school work while actively sending and receiving instant messages or while surfing the web? If so, what was the quality of your work? A recent nationwide survey found that over 40 percent of students reported that their school work suffered because of multitasking on the web. Are you in that 40 percent? If so, what are some ways that you can disconnect in order to get your work done? One suggestion is to find a quiet study spot and leave your computer in your room. If you can't leave your computer, room, or your Internet connection, consider purchasing software that will block digital distractions.

▶▶▶ BUILDING YOUR PORTFOLIO

What's in it for Me? Skills Matrix

Life is what happens to you while you're busy making other plans.
-John Lennon

How might the courses you are enrolled in right now affect your future? While it might be hard to imagine that there is a direct connection to your career or lifestyle after college, the classes and experiences you are engaged in now can play an important role in your future.

Developing a skills matrix will help you to reflect on your college experiences and track the skills that will help you land a great summer job, the hard-to-get internship, a scholarship, and one day, a career.

1. Create a new entry in your portfolio with the title "Skills Matrix." Record your work for this assignment there.

2. Begin by making a list of the skills you think you are acquiring or enhancing in the courses you are currently taking (e.g., critical thinking, writing, analysis).

   Tip: Course syllabi often list specific course goals—this is a good place to start.

3. Next, develop a skills matrix to identify courses and out-of-class experiences that enhance the following skills: communications, creativity, critical thinking, leadership, research, social responsibility, and teamwork. You might try using Microsoft Excel for the matrix. Identify three additional skill categories that you would like to track.

   - Include a "references" or "reflections' section for each course or experience.
   - Include important assignments/reflections in your portfolio for future reference.
   - Reflect on important experiences, noting what you learned, how the experience changed your thinking, your personal reaction, etc.

1. Save your skills matrix on your computer or external storage device.

2. Write a brief description of your skills matrix and then attach your worksheet to your description in your portfolio. Consider allowing your instructor and classmates to review the matrix and give you feedback.

3. Update your matrix often and include the revised version in your portfolio.

4. Use your reflections to connect knowledge with experiences in and out of class, on and off campus.

My First Semester {2008}

Skill Categories	Example (English 101)	Example (References)	(Course 2)	References	(Course 3)	References	(Out-of-Class Experience)	References	(Out-of-class activity 1)	References	(Out-of-class activity 2)	References	(Out-of-class activity 3)	References
Communications	X	Essay on Reading One: "Training on Real Life"												
Creativity	X	Creative writing project												
Critical Thinking														
Leadership														
Research	X	PowerPoint Presentation on Type Theory												
Social Responsibility														
Teamwork														
(new category)														
(new category)														

Thinking Critically:

Searching beyond Right and Wrong

Theodora Kalikow, president of the University of Maine at Farmington, describes the characteristics students should have in order to receive a good college education—which demands, above all else, critical thinking, the ability to think rationally:

- a flexible mind, able to move rapidly in new directions
- the ability to analyze a problem
- the ability to imagine solutions, to evaluate them by rational criteria or standards, and to commit to one of the solutions
- an understanding of how scholars in various academic fields conduct investigation

Critical thinking often involves examining things from a variety of perspectives.

- a skepticism of superficial arguments and easy solutions and a distrust of simplistic analysis
- a tolerance for ambiguity and complexity
- an ability to imagine and share the perceptions of different individuals, cultures, and times
- an appreciation of the community and one's place in it—the need to contribute to society through public and private service[1]

College has been described as "an investment in your future." This very appealing thought suggests that college not only can prepare you for a career but also can broaden your horizons in other ways.

A main ingredient in a college education is learning how to think critically. You'll explore different perspectives and you'll learn to make judgments using sound reasoning and multiple sources of evidence. If you believe that college is a path to a high-paying job, remember that a good critical thinker is a good job candidate. ■

---

[1]Theodora J. Kalikow, "Misconceptions about the Word 'Liberal' in Liberal Arts Education," *Higher Education and National Affairs* (June 8, 1998).

In this step you will learn:

- what critical thinking is and why there are no right and wrong answers to many important questions
- why critical thinking is an important lifelong skill
- what the four aspects of critical thinking are
- how you can avoid faulty reasoning
- how the college experience encourages critical thinking
- why and how you should critically evaluate information on the Internet

How Do You Measure Up?

Thinking Critically

Check the following items that apply to you:

_____ 1. I try to not allow my emotions to get in the way of making the right decision.

_____ 2. Even when I find some people irritating, I try to listen to what they have to say.

_____ 3. Whenever I have a good idea, I let it "sit on the back burner" before deciding to run with it.

_____ 4. I think that some questions have no one right answer.

_____ 5. I do my best to ask questions in class and participate in discussions.

_____ 6. I am careful to double-check information I find on the Internet to make sure it's legitimate.

_____ 7. I can recognize when facts just don't add up, even though they appear to be logical.

_____ 8. I am well aware that, as good as a textbook might be, it doesn't give me all the answers I need.

_____ 9. I believe that critical thinking is a desired skill with prospective employers.

_____ 10. My general education courses can help me become a better job candidate in almost any career field.

Review the items you did not check. Paying attention to all these aspects of your college experience can be very important to your success. After reading this step, come back to this list and choose an item or two that you did not check but are willing to work on.

Critical Thinking and Liberal Education

Most colleges and universities in the United States believe it's important to offer students what they call a "liberal" education. A liberal education has nothing to do with politics; rather it is defined as education that "enlarges and disciplines the mind" through exposure to different ideas and fields of study. Learning to think critically is at the core of a liberal education. Critical thinkers investigate all sides of a question and all possible solutions to a problem before reaching a conclusion or planning a course of action. They work hard to understand why some people believe one thing rather than another—whether or not they agree. Students who think critically ask relevant questions and test their assumptions against hard evidence.

If you lack critical thinking capabilities, you might exhibit behaviors similar to these:

- You're watching television and you see a commercial for a quick weight-loss pill. The commercial lists the "miracle" ingredients, promises that by taking the pill you'll lose ten pounds in two weeks, and offers a money-back guarantee. You pick up the phone and call in your order.
- You are asked to do research on the pros and cons of the electoral college. You look online and find two news articles about how the electoral college played a role in the controversial 2000 presidential race between George W. Bush and Al Gore. One article claims the electoral college system is outdated; the other defends that system. After reading the two opinions, you can't see how both sides can be right. But you don't know where and how to look for more evidence to support either position so you just decide to let your professor tell you which opinion is the right one.
- The instructor of your criminal justice class announces that students will be asked to debate capital punishment. You believe strongly in capital punishment and are very frustrated when you learn that you've been assigned to the team opposing it. You consider refusing to participate, even if it means a failing grade.

Now let's transform you into a critical thinker and look at some possible outcomes:

- You listen to the weight-loss commercial with interest but are doubtful about the claims. For another opinion, you talk to the wellness counselor on campus. She assures you that none of the ingredients could possibly have any effect on your weight, but she gives you suggestions for a diet and an exercise plan that are more likely to work.
- You compare the representation provided by the electoral college system with the representation provided by the popular vote, using library or Internet sources to find at least three articles defending each side. Now you have a number of things to write about. You find there isn't a clear-cut answer. That's okay. It's what you learned that counts.
- You would prefer not to oppose anything you believe in strongly, but you weigh your options and decide that you'll need to participate in the debate. You gather lots of information, and the books and articles you read introduce you to a different way of thinking. Although you still believe that capital punishment is a necessary deterrent, you begin to understand the other side of the argument and believe that you can do a good job of debating.

Collaboration Fosters Critical Thinking

A study by Professor Anuradha A. Gokhale at Western Illinois University, published in the fall 1995 issue of

Successful Critical Thinking

1. Practice collaborative learning because it helps develop critical thinking skills.
2. When making an argument, explore the subject fully through articles, books, and other reliable sources.
3. Keep in mind that uncertainty is often more healthy than certainty.
4. Continuously hone your critical thinking skills, because demonstrated critical thinking ability will enhance your marketability in practically any occupation.

the *Journal of Technology Education*, found that students who participated in collaborative learning—studying with others—performed significantly better on a test requiring critical thinking than students who studied individually.[2] It's easy to understand why: Students working together generate a greater number of thoughts than a student working alone. As a group learns to agree on the most reliable thoughts, it moves closer to a more accurate solution.

A Skill to Carry You Through Life

Employers hiring college graduates often say they want an individual who can find information, analyze it, organize it, draw conclusions from it, and present it convincingly to others. These skills rely on good critical thinking, which includes the ability to:

- manage and interpret information in a reliable way
- examine existing ideas and develop new ones
- pose logical arguments. In the context of critical thinking, the term *argument* refers not to an emotional confrontation but to reasons and information brought together in logical support of some idea.
- recognize reliable evidence and form well-reasoned conclusions

Walking Through the Process

When thinking about an argument, a good critical thinker considers questions such as the following:

- Is the information given in support of the argument true? For example, could it be possible that both the electoral college system and the popular vote system might be equally representative?
- Does the information really support the conclusion? If you determine that each system has its merits (the electoral college gives more voting power to the less-populated states, whereas the popular vote represents how the majority of voters feel), can you conclude that there may be a more sensible way to employ both systems in presidential elections?
- Do you need to withhold judgment until better evidence is available? Maybe you lack proof that a system that counts both the electoral vote and the popular vote would be more fair, because this alternative has never been tried.
- Is the argument truly based on good reasoning, or does it appeal mainly to your emotions? You may think the electoral vote can alter the results of

Employers strive to build a workforce empowered by strong critical thinkers.

elections in a way that undermines the intentions of the voters, as evidenced in the 2000 presidential election. But you need to ask whether your emotions, instead of relevant information that supports the argument, are guiding you to this conclusion.
- Based on the available evidence, are other conclusions equally likely (or even more likely)? Is there more than one right or possible answer? Perhaps there is a third or fourth way to count the vote by replacing the electoral college concept with something else.
- What more must you do to reach a good conclusion? You might need to do more reading about the electoral process and find evidence that the system didn't work as intended in earlier presidential elections. You might try to find out how people in those cases felt about the voting system.

Good critical thinking also involves thinking creatively about what assumptions may have been left out or what alternative conclusions may not have been considered. When communicating an argument or idea to others, a good critical thinker knows how to organize it in an understandable, convincing way in speech or in writing.

TRY IT!

Reflecting on Arguments

Do you tend to ask questions such as those in the "Walking through the Process" section when you read or when you listen to or take part in discussions? Each evening for the next week, revisit the list and think about whether you have asked such questions that day. If not, resolve to integrate these kinds of questions consistently into your learning.

---

[2]Anuradha Gokhale, "Collaborative Learning Enhances Critical Thinking," *Journal of Technology Education7*, no. 1 (1995).

Practicing Four Aspects of Critical Thinking—and Avoiding Faulty Reasoning

According to William T. Daly, a professor of political science at The Richard Stockton College of New Jersey, the critical thinking process can be divided into four basic steps. Although you should not expect to master critical thinking overnight, practicing these steps can help you become a more effective thinker.

1. *Abstract thinking: using details to discover a bigger idea.* From large numbers of facts, seek the bigger ideas, or the abstractions, behind the facts. What are the key ideas? Ask yourself what larger concepts the details suggest.

Let's say you read an article that describes how many people are using the Internet now, how much consumer information it provides, what kinds of goods you can buy cheaply over the Internet, and how there are many low-income families who still don't own computers. If you think carefully about these facts, you might arrive at several different important generalizations. One general conclusion might be that, as the Internet becomes even more important for shopping, families without a home computer will face ever greater disadvantages. Or your general idea might be that, because sales over the Internet have grown so explosively, companies will probably find a way to put a computer in every home.

2. *Creative thinking: seeking connections, finding new possibilities, rejecting nothing.* Use your general idea to see what further ideas it suggests. At this stage it's important not to reject any of your ideas. Write them all down. You'll narrow this list in the next step.

The creative phase of thinking can lead you from your general idea into many directions. Returning to our example of the Internet article, one path might involve searching for ways to make the Internet more available to low-income households. Another approach might be to investigate how much interest big companies really have in marketing various goods to low-income families. In essence, the creative thinking stage involves developing the general idea—finding new ways to apply it or identifying other ideas it might suggest.

3. *Systematic thinking: organizing the possibilities, tossing out the rubbish.* When you practice systematic thinking, you look at the outcome of the creative thinking phase in a rigorous, critical way. This is the stage where you narrow the list. If you are looking for solutions to a problem, which ones seem most promising after you have done your research? Do some answers conflict with others? Which ones can be achieved? If you have found new evidence to refine or further test your generalization, what does that new evidence show? Does your original generalization still hold up? Do you need to modify it? What further conclusions do good reasoning and evidence support? Which notions should you abandon?

4. *Precise communication: presenting your ideas convincingly to others.* Intelligent conclusions aren't useful if you cannot share them with others. Consider what your audience will need to know to follow your reasoning and be persuaded. Have your facts in hand as you attempt to convince others of the truth of your argument. Don't be defensive; be logical.

Avoiding Logical Fallacies

You may believe you've reached a conclusion or solved a problem logically but later find yourself a victim of faulty reasoning. The following fallacies will prevent you from thinking critically or correctly. Avoid them.

Challenging the person, not the argument When you challenge others' positions, make sure it's their arguments you're challenging, not the individuals themselves. In instances of a controversial or an emotional

© Comstock Select/Corbis

When you challenge someone else's position, take care to challenge the argument, not the person.

Begging "Please, officer, don't give me a ticket, because if you do I'll lose my license. I don't deserve to lose my license because I have five children to feed and won't be able to if I can't drive my truck." None of the driver's statements offer any evidence, in any legal sense, as to why he shouldn't be given a ticket. The driver is begging for pity.

Appealing to authority When you base your argument on the opinion of someone who may or may not be an authority on the topic, you rely on the appearance of authority rather than on real evidence. Students frequently fall into the authority trap by putting great weight on what other students say about instructors or courses or by consulting a friend about proper answers for a class assignment.

Letting beauty or popularity sway your opinion Studies by psychologists indicate that we believe more what successful and attractive people tell us than what those who aren't so successful or attractive say. One of the worst kinds of reasoning you can follow is to base your arguments on a person's looks or popularity.

Believing something is true because it hasn't been proved false Large bookstores typically offer dozens of books detailing close encounters with flying saucers and beings from outer space. All of these books describe the person who has had the encounter as beyond reproach in integrity and sanity. Because critics have not disproved the witnesses' claims, the events "really occurred." Even in science, few things are ever proved completely false, but evidence can be discredited.

Falling victim to false cause Frequently, we think that just because one event was followed by another, the first event must have caused the second. Too often, students blame their failure on the instructor when they are in fact responsible for their own nonsuccess. Blaming your instructor when you don't take notes in class, don't review them, and don't compile notes as you read is an example of the fallacy of false cause.

Making hasty generalizations Reaching a conclusion in a research paper based on the opinion of one source is like concluding that all the marbles in the barrel of one hundred marbles are green after pulling out just one marble. Don't jump into similarly hasty generalizations in your courses. Don't assume, either, that just because one course you took in sociology or biology was boring, all courses in those subjects will be boring.

question, such as the legality of abortion, it's easy to get caught up with the character or reputation of an opponent rather than with the content of the opponent's argument.

Using a threat to win an argument Your parents may pressure you to agree they are right on some issue by suggesting that, unless you make such an admission, you might not receive your monthly allowance. A student might employ such a tactic against an instructor by threatening to give the instructor a poor evaluation. An instructor might use a similar approach with students by threatening to fail them for not agreeing with her.

How College Encourages Critical Thinking

If you are like many college students, you might believe that your instructors will have all the answers. Unfortunately, most important questions do not have simple answers, and in your college experience you will discover numerous ways to look at important issues. In any event, you must be willing to challenge assumptions and conclusions, even those presented by experts. To challenge how you think, a good college instructor may insist that the method for solving a problem is as important as the solution, and even may ask you to describe your problem-solving process.

Because critical thinking depends on discovering and testing connections between ideas, your instructor may ask open-ended questions that have no clear-cut answers, questions of "Why?" "How?" or "What if?" For example, an instructor might say: "In these essays we have two conflicting ideas about whether bilingual education is effective in helping children learn English. What now?" She may ask you to break a larger question into smaller ones: "Let's take the first point. What evidence does the author offer for his idea that English language immersion programs get better results?" The instructor may insist that more than one valid point of view exists: "So, for some types of students, do you agree that bilingual education might be best? What other types of students should we consider?" She may require you to explain concretely the reason for any point you reject: "You think this essay is flawed. Well, what are your reasons?" Or she may challenge the authority of experts: "Dr. Fleming's theory sounds impressive. But here are some facts he doesn't account for. . . ." You may discover that often your instructor reinforces what you think about a topic: "So something like this happened to you once, and you felt

exactly the same way. Can you tell us why?" And you will come to understand that you can change your mind and that it's acceptable to do so.

Your instructor may ask you to consider the issue of national health care. He may ask you to research the number of U. S. citizens who have no health insurance in comparison to other Western countries. What are the trade-offs between providing health care for

© Comstock/Corbis

Your professors will find many ways to stimulate and challenge your thinking.

Observing How Instructors Challenge Your Thinking

Think about your experiences in your classes so far this term, and answer these questions:

- Have your instructors pointed out any conflicts or contradictions in the ideas they have presented? Or have you noted any contradictions that they have not acknowledged?

- Have they asked questions for which they sometimes don't seem to have the answers? Give concrete examples.

- Have they challenged you or other members of the class to explain yourselves more fully? In what ways?

everyone and increased taxation? Is there any evidence that a national health care system will reduce freedom of choice when considering health care providers? What about the quality of health care? He may require you to support your opinion that the "U. S. health care system is the best in the world." He may also ask you to consider the ethical issues related to health care costs—if the government bears all the cost for health care, will choices have to be made about who lives and who dies? Are some of those choices being made already by private insurance companies?

You might find thinking like this difficult at first. You may also discover that answers are seldom entirely wrong or right but are more often somewhere in between. Yet the questions that lack simple answers usually are the most important ones. If you accept this way of thinking, your classes won't necessarily be easier, but they certainly will be more interesting, because you will know how to use logic to figure things out instead of depending purely on how you feel or what you've heard.

A good class becomes a critical thinking experience. As you listen to the instructor, try to predict where the lecture is heading and why. When other students bring up issues, ask yourself whether they have enough information to justify what they have said. And when you raise your hand to participate, remember that asking a sensible question may be more important than trying to present the elusive "right" answer.

The best way to practice and develop critical thinking skills is to take demanding college courses that provide a variety of opportunities to think out loud, to discuss and interact in class, and especially to do research and write. When your instructors use essay examinations instead of multiple-choice, true/false, and short-answer exams, you will be much more likely to develop your critical thinking skills.

Where to Go for Help On Campus

Logic courses: Check out your philosophy department's course in introduction to logic. This may be the single best course for learning critical thinking skills.

Argument courses and critical thinking courses: Argument courses are usually offered in the English department. They will help you develop the ability to formulate logical arguments and to avoid such pitfalls as logical fallacies.

Debating skills: Some of the best critical thinkers have participated in debating during college. Go to either your student activities office or your department of speech/drama and find out if your campus has a debate club/society or a debate team.

Critically Evaluating Information on the Internet

Anyone can put anything on the Internet. It is often difficult to tell where material on the Internet originated, how it got there, and who wrote it. The lack of proper citation—statement of authorship—makes it difficult to judge the credibility of the information. So the first thing to do when using any Internet source is to look for a citation. Then, using the citation, search for the original source and evaluate its authenticity. If there is no citation, chances are you should avoid the site. Ask yourself these questions:

- Is the material credible? Is it the original? Is it quoted out of context? Is it plagiarized—that is, passed off as one's own instead of cited with the true source? Is it altered—intentionally or unintentionally—from the original? Have experts reviewed the material?

© PhotoDisc/Ryon McVey/Getty Images

It's crucial to establish the credibility and accuracy of information you find on the Internet.

- Who is the author? What can you find out about the author? Is the author qualified to write this article? If you can't find information about the author, think twice before using the material. Beware of sites that have no date on the material, make sweeping generalizations, and use information that is biased and does not acknowledge opposing views.
- Does it reflect mainstream opinions? Whether you're looking for a fact, an opinion, or some advice, it is a good idea to find at least three sources that agree. If the sources do not agree, do further research to find out the range of opinion or disagreement before you draw your conclusions. If the site is sponsored by an advocacy group, be aware of the group's agenda or cause; it will affect the reliability of the information.[3]

How and Where to Check the Accuracy of Online Information

Double-check the author's affiliation and credentials by looking at other online references and directories. For instance, if an author claims to be a university professor or member of a prestigious organization, check the specific organization websites to verify that affiliation. Look for other works by the author. Read a few of them. How accurate and unbiased do they sound?

Most print matter (books, articles, and so forth) has been reviewed (vetted) by an editorial board. Frequently it's difficult to confirm that the same is true for information on an Internet source, with some exceptions. For example, if you are searching through a major national database such as the Human Genome Database, the Civil War Database, or ERIC, the Education Resources Information Center, it is highly likely that sources from these important collections have been reviewed.

Of course, you may use Internet search engines, too. But you should compare the information you find

---

[3]Adapted from Robert Harris, "Evaluating Internet Research Sources," VirtualSalt. 17 Nov. 1997. (**http://www.virtualsalt.com/evalu8it.htm**.) Reprinted by permission.

with information from print sources or at least two other vetted electronic databases.

Nine Suggestions for Evaluating Internet Sources

On its website (**http://www.uwec.edu/Library/ guides/tencs.html**), the McIntyre Library at the University of Wisconsin–Eau Claire offers these additional suggestions for checking Internet sources:

- **Content** What is the intent of the content? Are the title and author identified? Is the content regularly reviewed by experts? Is the content popular or scholarly, satiric or serious? What is the date of the document or article? Is the information current? Do you have the latest version? (Is this important?) How do you know?
- **Credibility** Is the author identifiable and reliable? Is the content credible? Authoritative? Should it be? What is the purpose of the information? Is the URL extension .edu, .com, .gov, or .org? What does the extension tell you about the provider of the information?
- **Critical Thinking** How can you apply critical thinking skills, including previous knowledge and experience, to evaluate Internet resources? Can you identify the author, provider of the information, date of the information, and so on as you could for a traditionally published resource? What criteria do you use to evaluate Internet resources?
- **Copyright** The copyright notice should appear prominently. Why? Because someone wrote, or is responsible for, the creation of a document, graphic, sound, or an image, and the material falls under the copyright rules. Fair use applies to the borrowing of short, cited excerpts, usually as examples to support an author's own argument or for the purposes of a critical review or research. Materials may be in the public domain—that is, they are public property, unprotected by copyright, and available for anyone to reproduce freely—if the website explicitly says so. Internet users, like consumers of print media, must respect copyright.

- **Citation** Internet resources should be cited to identify sources used, both to give credit to the author and to provide the reader with avenues for further research. Standard style manuals (print and online) provide examples of how to cite Internet documents, although these standards are not uniform.
- **Continuity** Will the Internet site be maintained and updated? Is it now and will it continue to be free? Can you rely on this source over time to provide up-to-date information? Some good .edu sites have moved to .com, with possible cost implications. Other sites offer temporary or partial use for free and charge fees for continued or in-depth use.
- **Censorship** If you are participating in an Internet listserv, is the list open or moderated? Messages posted to a moderated list are reviewed by a moderator before they are distributed to the entire list. Does your search engine or index look for all words, or are some words excluded? Is this censorship? Does your institution, based on its mission, parent organization, or space limitations, apply some restrictions to Internet use? Consider censorship and privacy issues when using the Internet.
- **Comparability** Does the Internet resource have an identified comparable print or electronic data set or source? Does the Internet site contain comparable and complete information? (For example, some newspapers have partial but not full text information on the Internet.) Do you need to compare data or statistics over time? Can you identify sources for comparable earlier or later data? Comparability of data may or may not be important, depending on your project.
- **Context** What is the context (frame of reference) for your research? Can you find commentary, opinion, narrative, statistics, and so forth? Are you looking for current or historical information? Definitions? Research studies or articles? How does Internet information fit in the overall information context of your subject? Before you start searching, define the research context and research needs, and determine your optimal sources for filling your information needs without data overload.

WIRED WINDOW

BLOGS ALLOW ANYONE, even those with limited web-publishing experience, to post online journals that look professional. Blogs emerged in 2003 and their popularity has only increased, with Internet users creating over 100,000 new blogs every day. Because there are so many blogs, they cover just about any topic you can think of—from politics to purchasing, movies to money, sex to Silicone Valley. If you want to know a blogger's opinion about anything, you can find it in the blogosphere. Because there are so many blogs, opinions about an issue can range widely among bloggers, with some supporting a certain viewpoint, some being against it, and many others being somewhere in between. To sharpen your critical thinking skills, Google a current event that you find interesting. Next, search for blogs with commentary on the topic. (Hint: search for the topic keywords plus the word "blog.") Find two blogs with different viewpoints on the same topic. To help you, review the four aspects of critical thinking and answer the following questions: What is each blogger's viewpoint? Do the people who leave comments generally agree or disagree with the blogger's point of view? Why does the blogger hold that point of view? Is there any evidence on the blog that supports the blogger's view? Do you have any opinion on the topic? Which blogger do you most agree with? Why?

Think

▶▶▶ BUILDING YOUR PORTFOLIO

My Influences

We all take different paths in life, but no matter
where we go, we take a little of each other everywhere.

-Tim McGraw (b. 1967), American country music singer

Our past experiences shape the way we think and perceive the world around us. Sometimes it is easy to interpret things without stopping to think about why we feel the way we do. How have people or events shaped the way you see the world today?

For this activity, you will create a new entry in your portfolio with the title "My Influences." You will insert photos of people (family, friends, celebrities, national leaders) and events (a personal experience or local/national/international event) that have affected your worldview. Beneath each photo, write a description and a reflection based on the questions/model below.

1. Describe how the people you select have influenced you.

Upload photo here.	Upload photo here.	Upload photo here.

_____

_____

_____

_____

_____

_____

_____

_____

Maximizing Your
Learning Success:

Engaging with Learning and Making the Most of Your Learning Style

© Chip East/Reuters/CORBIS

**In some courses, learning occ
in your body as well as your mind**

Research reveals that students who become genuinely engaged in their college experience have a greater chance of success than those who do not. "Engagement" means participating actively in your academic life and approaching every challenge with determination. One way to begin is to get to know your instructors, especially those who offer you the chance to learn actively. Whenever your instructor asks you a question in class, assigns groups to solve a problem, or requires you to make an oral presentation to the class, you become actively engaged in learning. Learning should be not only easier but also more rewarding and successful as a result.

To do well in college, it is also important to understand and use your preferred learning style. Experts agree that there is no one best way to learn. You may have trouble listening to a long lecture, or listening may be the way you learn best. You may love classroom discussion, or you may consider hearing other students' opinions a waste of time.

You've probably already discovered that college instructors and even courses also have their own particular styles. Many instructors rely almost solely on lecturing, whereas others use lots of visual aids. In science courses, you'll conduct experiments or go on field trips where you can observe or touch what you are studying. In dance, theater, and physical education, learning takes place in your body and your mind. And in almost all courses, you'll also learn by reading both textbooks and other materials. You'll find some professors friendly and warm, whereas others will seem to want little interaction with students. It's safe to say that in at least some of your college courses, you won't find a close match between the way you learn most effectively and the way you're being taught.

This step will help you engage actively with your coursework, classmates, and instructors and will ask you to complete a learning inventory to shed light on how you learn best. It will examine common learning disabilities and offer advice and resources for treating them. The knowledge and insights you gain should help you get the most out of your learning and maximize the "return" on your college investment. ■

In this step you will learn:

- how being an engaged learner and a collaborative learner helps you not only to learn more effectively but also to enjoy your college experience more

- what strategies you can use to form high-quality learning teams

- how study groups are particularly helpful for science and math classes

- how you can work most effectively with your instructors and get the greatest benefit out of the student–instructor relationship

- how you can use a learning styles inventory to determine your preferred mode of learning, and apply the results to studying and learning

- what some common types of learning disabilities are and how you can recognize them in yourself or others

How Do You Measure Up?

Maximizing Your Learning Success

Check the following items that apply to you:

____ 1. I think there are many ways to learn beyond listening and reading.

____ 2. I know which of my senses I use most frequently in learning.

____ 3. I understand the benefits of studying in groups.

____ 4. I know the advantages of having strong, positive relationships with faculty.

____ 5. I can identify which of my classes are taught in ways that allow me to use my preferred style of learning.

____ 6. I know what to do if I can't adjust to a professor's teaching style.

____ 7. I have developed ways to use all my strengths in the learning process.

____ 8. I understand which of my current courses ask me to learn in different ways.

____ 9. I can identify students in at least some of my classes who learn the same way I do, and some who learn in different ways.

____ 10. I can recognize the signs of common learning disabilities, and I know where to get help with a learning problem I might have.

Review the items you did not check. Paying attention to all these aspects of your college experience can be very important to your success. After reading this step, come back to this list and choose an item or two that you did not check but are willing to work on.

Engaging with Learning

Engaging with learning requires you to prepare before and after every class, not just before exams. You might need to do library research, make appointments to talk with faculty members, prepare outlines from your class notes, ask someone to read your written assignment to see if it's clear, or have a serious discussion with students whose personal values are different from yours. This active approach to learning has the potential to make you well rounded in all aspects of your life. With good active-learning skills, you will feel more comfortable socially, gain a greater appreciation for diversity and education, and be better able to clarify your academic major and future career.

Collaborative Learning Teams

More than likely, you'll be working with others after college, so now is a good time to learn how to collaborate. Students who engage in learning through a team approach not only learn better but often enjoy their learning experiences more. Whether on teams or by themselves, engaged learners are willing to try new ideas and discover new knowledge by exploring the world around them instead of just memorizing facts.

Joseph Cuseo of Marymount College, an expert on collaborative learning, points to these advantages of learning teams:

- Learners learn from one another as well as from the instructor.
- Collaborative learning is by its nature active learning, and so it tends to increase learning through engagement.
- "Two heads are better than one." Collaboration can lead to more ideas, alternative approaches, new perspectives, and better solutions.
- If you're uneasy about speaking out in large classes, you will tend to be more comfortable participating in small groups, and better communication and better ideas will result.
- You will develop stronger bonds with other students in the class, which may increase everyone's interest in attending.
- "Positive competition" among groups happens when several groups are asked to solve the same problem—with the instructor clarifying that the purpose is for the good of all.

- Working in teams may help you develop leadership skills.[1]

Making learning teams productive Not all learning teams are equally effective. Sometimes teamwork fails to reach its potential because no thought was given to how the group was formed or how it should function. Use the following strategies to develop high-quality learning teams that maximize the power of peer collaboration:

1. Use learning teams for more than just preparing for exams. Effective student learning teams collaborate regularly for other academic tasks besides test review sessions.
2. Seek out team members who will contribute quality and diversity to the group. Resist the urge to limit the group to people who are just like you. Look for students who are motivated, attend class regularly, are attentive and participate actively while in class, and complete assignments.
3. Keep the team small (four to six teammates). Small groups allow for more face-to-face interaction and eye contact and less opportunity for any one individual to shirk responsibility to the team.
4. Hold individual team members personally accountable for contributing to the learning of their teammates. One way to ensure accountability is to have each member come to group meetings with specific information or answers to share with teammates, as well as with questions to ask the group.

The many uses of learning teams Learning teams can serve a number of valuable purposes:

- **Note-taking teams.** Team up with other students immediately after class to share and compare notes so that your group may still have a chance to consult with the instructor about any missing or confusing information.
- **Reading teams.** After completing reading assignments, team with other students to compare your highlighting and margin notes. See if all agree.
- **Library research teams.** Develop a support group for reducing "library anxiety" and for locating and

---

[1]Joseph Cuseo, *Igniting Student Involvement, Peer Interaction, and Teamwork: A Taxonomy of Specific Cooperative Learning Structures and Collaborative Learning Strategies* (Stillwater, OK: New Forums Press, 2002).

© Digital Vision/Getty Images

Learning teams are most effective when the group is small.

sharing sources of information (which does not constitute cheating or plagiarizing as long as the final product you turn in represents your own work).

- **Team/instructor conferences.** Schedule a time for your learning team to visit the instructor during office hours as needed to seek additional assistance.
- **Team review of test results.** After receiving test results, join with your team to review your individual tests together. Help one another identify the sources of mistakes, and share any answers that received high scores.
- **Teams for returning students.** If you are returning to college after a hiatus, you and other returning students may wish to form your own group and discuss the differences between your lives before college and now; or you may prefer to join a group of recent high school graduates to hear and provide different points of view.

Using Learning Teams in Mathematics and Science

Although working with students in a learning team is important for all courses, a learning team that serves as a study group is especially effective in science and math. In his groundbreaking research on the factors that predict success in calculus, Professor Uri Treisman of the University of Texas at Austin determined that the most effective strategy for success in calculus turned out to be active participation in a study group! It is now widely accepted that, by working together, a group of students can significantly enhance each other's performance, particularly in problem-solving

courses and especially when one member of the group is an advanced math student.

It seems that the larger the class and the more complex the material, the more valuable the study group. Although Treisman-style workshops in calculus, chemistry, physics, and other subjects have been established by schools across the country, most study groups are informal and organized by students themselves. Study groups work best when members take their commitment to each other seriously, make faithful attendance a priority, and set specific goals for each session.

Besides guiding you toward the solution to difficult problems, a math or science study group can help you and your team to:

Compare notes from class Look at the level of detail in each other's notes, and adopt the best of each other's styles. Discuss places where you got lost in an example problem. Talk about technical terms and symbols you didn't understand or couldn't decipher on the board, and ask about questions raised in class that you didn't completely understand.

Teach each other Split up the difficult problems and assign them to various members to prepare and present to the group. Remember that the best way to learn something is to explain it to someone else.

Prepare for tests Divide the job of making a study outline. Each person brings his or her section. Team members discuss and modify the outlines, and a final version is created for all. Group members can quiz one another, focusing on facts and specific pieces of information for an objective test and on the relationship of those pieces to one another for an essay exam. Members then can write practice questions for each other, or the group might create an entire sample exam and take it together under timed conditions.

Provide makeup notes If you absolutely have to miss a math or science class, consult with members of your study group for notes and the assignment. Catch up before the next class. Otherwise you will get further and further behind.

Ask the right questions Never criticize a question in your study group; respond positively and express appreciation for all contributions. If you notice someone is lost, give that person an opportunity to ask a question by reviewing the work: "Let's see if we all understand what we've done so far. . . ." If you are explaining your solution to a problem, try leading the others through it by asking a series of simple questions. Above all, come to the group meeting prepared—not with all the answers, but knowing what specific questions you have.

Working with Your College Instructors

Some of your greatest opportunities for learning in college will come from one-on-one time with faculty members outside of class. Professors post the office hours when they're available to help students; make an appointment to see them during that time. Don't feel as if you're bothering them. It's part of their job to make time for you.

You can do a few simple things to establish good relations between you and your instructors:

- Come to class regularly and on time.
- Take advantage of office hours to get to know your instructors.
- Read the assigned material before class.
- Ask questions.
- Sit near the front of the class. Studies show that students who do so tend to earn better grades.
- Make sure that you are civil and respectful during class. Make sure you don't talk on your cell phone or use your laptop inappropriately or for tasks unrelated to what's going on in class.
- Never talk or whisper to other students while instructors are lecturing. They may interpret this behavior as inconsiderate or even disrespectful.
- Don't hand your professors phony excuses. Many of them can spot a lie a mile away. If you're sincere and you give honest reasons for missing class or an assignment, your professors are more likely to work with you.

Some things that college instructors do may be new to your learning experience. These may include:

- supplementing textbook assignments with other reading
- giving exams that cover both assigned readings and lectures
- questioning the conclusions of various scholars
- accepting several different student opinions on a question
- never checking to see whether you are taking notes or reading the text

Take advantage of your professors' office hours to get help when you need it and to establish a positive relationship with them.

- requiring that you do extensive reading in a short period of time
- giving fewer quizzes than high school teachers give

A Good Instructor Wants You to Succeed

Your instructors want you to succeed. As a result, they may work you harder than you're accustomed to. They also may be demanding, quick to disagree with your ideas, and ready to correct you when you answer a question incorrectly in class. Yet getting to know your professors and establishing a positive relationship with them can be one of the most rewarding experiences of your life.

To learn more about your instructors, you might begin by observing their offices. You will usually find their work space decorated to reflect their interests and personality. Professors read extensively and like to talk about what they have read. Some may speak of travels abroad or to other parts of the United States where they have lived, taught, or conducted research.

You might be surprised to learn that most college faculty members never have taken a course in teaching.

Instead, they chose courses in their fields of study to acquire and understand new knowledge. Some have left nonteaching careers in order to teach college students about those careers and their subject matter: You'll find former lawyers teaching law, former physicians teaching medicine, former newspaper editors teaching journalism, and former executives teaching business management.

If things go wrong between you and an instructor What if you can't tolerate a particular professor or adjust to her teaching style? Arrange a meeting to try to work things out. Getting to know the instructor may help you cope with the way she teaches the course. If that fails, check the drop/add date. You may have to drop the course altogether and add a different one. If it's too late to add classes, you may still want to drop by the drop date later in the term and avoid a poor or failing grade. See your academic adviser or counselor for help with this decision.

If you can't resolve the situation with the instructor and need to stay in the class, see the head of the department. If you are still dissatisfied, move up the administrative ladder until you get a definite answer. Never allow a bad professor to sour you on college. If all else fails, even the worst course will be over in a matter of weeks.

What if you're not satisfied with your grade on an assignment? First, make an appointment to see the instructor and discuss the assignment. She may give you a second chance because you took the time to ask for help. If you get a low grade on an exam, you might ask the professor to review certain answers with you. Never demand a grade change, as this request most likely will backfire.

Where to Go for Help: Learning

On Campus

Learning (assistance/support) center: Almost every campus has one or more of these. Sometimes they provide help for students in all subjects at all levels; sometimes they are specific to one discipline. The staff will know many, if not all, of your instructors and can provide good advice for using active-learning strategies.

These centers typically retain outstanding undergraduate students who serve as tutors. From their experiences, they can teach you how to make active learning easier and more enjoyable. Above all, remember: Learning centers are not just for students who are having academic trouble—they are for all students who want to improve their learning skills.

Counseling center: Maybe your courses and your relationships with your instructors are putting you under excessive stress—a fairly common issue among new college students. There's help right on campus at the counseling center, which provides free and confidential support for students. You can get feedback on the sources of your stress and learn new coping mechanisms. You already have paid for such services in your basic tuition and fees. Seeking a counselor simply means that, as a new student with concerns, you are taking steps to get the assistance you need.

Faculty members: Probably some of your professors strike you as approachable and sympathetic. Make an appointment to see one of them and share your concerns.

Academic adviser/counselor: Make a special effort to meet your adviser/counselor, especially if you're having problems in any of your courses or if circumstances are keeping you from earning higher grades. If you don't feel comfortable with your adviser, you have the right to ask for a new one.

Online

Active Learning: Creating Excitement in the Classroom: **http://www.ntlf.com/html/lib/bib/91-9dig.htm**. Check out the authors' interpretation of the active-learning process.

Tools for Teaching: http://teaching.berkeley.edu/bgd/ collaborative.html. Read the information designed for instructors on collaborative learning.

Learning How You Learn Best: The VARK Learning Styles Inventory

At the beginning of this step, we stated that college success depends on knowing and using your most effective learning style. There are many models for thinking about and describing learning styles. Of dozens of such approaches, we focus here on one popular model—the VARK—and we present its learning styles inventory to help you to determine your best mode of learning.

The VARK (Visual, Aural, Read/Write, and Kinesthetic) Learning Styles Inventory

Unlike learning styles theories that rely on personality or intelligence, the VARK focuses on how learners prefer to use their senses to learn. The acronym VARK stands for "Visual," "Aural," "Read/Write," and "Kinesthetic." Visual learners prefer to learn information through charts, graphs, symbols, and other visual means. Aural learners favor hearing information. Read/Write learners prefer to learn information that is displayed as words. Kinesthetic learners are most comfortable learning through experience and practice, whether simulated or real. To determine your learning style according to the VARK Inventory, respond to the questionnaire that follows.

The VARK Questionnaire

(Version 7.0, 2006)

Choose the answers which best explain your preference and circle the letters next to it. Please circle more than one if a single answer does not match your perception. Leave blank any question that does not apply.

1. You are helping someone who wants to go to your airport, town center or railway station. You would:
   a) draw or give her a map.
   b) tell her the directions.
   c) write down the directions as a list.
   d) go with her.

2. You are not sure whether a word should be spelled "dependent" or "dependant." You would:
   a) see the words in your mind and choose by the way they look.
   b) think about how each word sounds and choose one.
   c) find it in a dictionary.
   d) write both words on paper and choose one.

3. You are planning a holiday for a group. You want some feedback from the group about your plan. You would:
   a) use a map or website to show them the places.
   b) phone, text, or email them.
   c) give them a copy of the printed itinerary.
   d) describe some of the highlights.

4. You are going to cook something as a special treat for your family. You would:
   a) look through the cookbook for ideas from the pictures.
   b) ask friends for suggestions.
   c) use a cookbook where you know there is a good recipe.
   d) cook something you know without the need for instructions.

5. A group of tourists wants to learn about the parks or wildlife reserves in your area. You would:
   a) show them Internet pictures, photographs, or picture books.
   b) talk about, or arrange a talk for them about parks or wildlife reserves.
   c) give them a book or pamphlets about the parks or wildlife reserves.
   d) take them to a park or wildlife reserve and walk with them.

6. You are about to purchase a digital camera or mobile phone. Other than price, what would most influence your decision?

   a) It is a modern design and looks good.

   b) The salesperson telling you about its features.

   c) Reading the details about its features.

   d) Trying or testing it.

7. Remember a time when you learned how to do something new. Try to avoid choosing a physical skill, (e.g., riding a bike). You learned best by:

   a) diagrams and charts—visual clues.

   b) listening to somebody explaining it and asking questions.

   c) written instructions (e.g., a manual or textbook).

   d) watching a demonstration.

8. You have a problem with your knee. You would prefer that the doctor:

   a) show you a diagram of what was wrong.

   b) describe what was wrong.

   c) give you a web address or something to read about it.

   d) use a plastic model of a knee to show what was wrong.

9. You want to learn a new program, skill, or game on a computer. You would:

   a) follow the diagrams in the book that came with it.

   b) talk with people who know about the program.

   c) read the written instructions that came with the program.

   d) use the controls or keyboard.

10. You like websites that have:

   a) interesting design and visual features.

   b) audio channels where you can hear music, radio programs, or interviews.

   c) interesting written descriptions, lists, and explanations.

   d) things you can click on, shift, or try.

11. Other than price, what would most influence your decision to buy a new non-fiction book?

   a) The way it looks is appealing.

   b) A friend talks about it and recommends it.

   c) Quickly reading parts of it.

   d) It has real-life stories, experiences, and examples.

12. You are using a book, CD, or website to learn how to take photos with your new digital camera. You would like to have:

   a) diagrams showing the camera and what each part does.

   b) a chance to ask questions and talk about the camera and its features.

   c) clear written instructions with lists and bullet points about what to do.

   d) many examples of good and poor photos and how to improve them.

13. Do you prefer a teacher or a presenter who uses:

   a) diagrams, charts or graphs?

   b) question-and-answer sessions, group discussion, or guest speakers?

   c) handouts, books, or readings?

   d) demonstrations, models, or practical sessions?

14. You have finished a competition or test and would like some feedback. You would like to have feedback:

   a) using graphs showing what you had achieved.

   b) from somebody who talks it through with you.

   c) using a written description of your results.

   d) using examples from what you have done.

15. You are going to choose food at a restaurant or cafe. You would:

   a) look at what others are eating or look at pictures of each dish.

   b) listen to the waiter or ask friends to recommend choices.

   c) choose from the descriptions in the menu.

   d) choose something that you have had there before.

16. You have to make an important speech at a conference or special occasion. You would:

   a) make diagrams or get graphs to help explain things.

   b) write a few key words and practice saying your speech over and over.

   c) write out your speech and learn from reading it over several times.

   d) gather many examples and stories to make the talk real and practical.

Copyright Version 7.0 (2006) held by Neil D. Fleming, Christchurch, New Zealand and Charles C. Bonwell, Green Mountain Falls, Colorado 80819 U.S.A.

Scoring the VARK

Use the following scoring chart to find the VARK category that each of your answers corresponds to. Circle the letters that correspond to your answers. For example, if you answered b and c for question 3, circle V and R in the question 3 row.

Question	A category	B category	C category	D category
3	K	V	R	A

Learn

Scoring Chart

Question	A category	B category	C category	D category
1	K	A	R	V
2	V	A	R	K
3	K	V	R	A
4	K	A	V	R
5	A	V	K	R
6	K	R	V	A
7	K	A	V	R
8	R	K	A	V
9	R	A	K	V
10	K	V	R	A
11	V	R	A	K
12	A	R	V	K
13	K	A	R	V
14	K	R	A	V
15	K	A	R	V
16	V	A	R	K

Count the number of each of the VARK letters you have circled to get your score for each VARK category.

Total number of **V**s circled = _____

Total number of **A**s circled = _____

Total number of **R**s circled = _____

Total number of **K**s circled = _____

Scoring VARK

Because you could choose more than one answer for each question, the scoring is not just a simple matter of counting. It is like four stepping stones across some water. Enter your scores **from highest to lowest** on the stones below, with their V, A, R, and K labels.

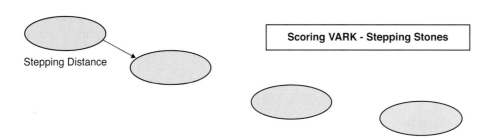

Stepping Distance

Scoring VARK - Stepping Stones

Your stepping distance comes from this table.

The total of my four VARK scores is -	My stepping distance is
16–21	1
22–27	2
28–32	3
More than 32	4

Follow these steps to establish your preferences.

1. Your first preference is always your highest score. Check that first stone as one of your preferences.
2. Now subtract your second highest score from your first. If that figure is larger than your stepping distance you have a single preference. Otherwise check this stone as another preference and continue with Step 3 below.
3. Subtract your third score from your second one. If that figure is larger than your stepping distance you have a bi-modal preference. If not, check your third stone as a preference and continue with Step 4 below.
4. Lastly, subtract your fourth score from your third one. If that figure is larger than your stepping distance you have a tri-modal preference. Otherwise, check your fourth stone as a preference and you have all four modes as your preferences!

Note: If you are bi-modal, tri-modal, or have checked all four modes as your preferences you can be described as *multi-modal* in your VARK preferences.

Using VARK Results to Study More Effectively

How can knowing your VARK score help you do better in your college classes? Here are ways of using learning styles to develop your own study strategies:

- If you have a visual learning preference, underline or highlight your notes, use symbols, charts, or graphs to display your notes, use different arrangements of words on the page, and redraw your pages from memory.
- If you are an aural learner, talk with others to verify the accuracy of your lecture notes. Put your notes on tape and listen or tape class lectures. Read your notes out loud; ask yourself questions and speak your answers.
- If you have a read/write learning preference, write and rewrite your notes, and read your notes silently. Organize diagrams or flow charts into statements, and write imaginary exam questions and respond in writing.
- If you are a kinesthetic learner, you will need to use all your senses in learning—sight, touch, taste, smell, and hearing. Supplement your notes with real-world examples; move and gesture while you are reading or speaking your notes.

Learn

Learning with a Learning Disability

While everyone has a learning style, a portion of the population has what is characterized as a "learning disability." Learning disabilities are usually recognized and diagnosed in grade school. But occasionally students successfully compensate for a learning problem and reach college never having been properly diagnosed or assisted.

What Is a Learning Disability (LD)?

A learning disability (LD) is a disorder that affects people's ability either to interpret what they see and hear or to link information from different parts of the brain. These limitations can show up as specific difficulties with spoken and written language, coordination, self-control, or attention. Such difficulties can impede learning to read, write, or do math. Because "LD" is a broad term that covers a range of possible causes, symptoms, treatments, and outcomes, it is difficult to diagnose or to pinpoint the causes. The types of LD that most commonly affect college students are disorders in academic skills, such as developmental reading, writing, and mathematics.

Dyslexia, a developmental reading disorder, is quite widespread. A person with dyslexia can have problems with any of the tasks involved in reading. However, scientists have found that a significant number of people with dyslexia share an inability to distinguish or separate the sounds in spoken words. For instance, dyslexic individuals sometimes have difficulty assigning the appropriate sounds to letters either by themselves or in combination when they form words. Yet there is more to reading than recognizing words. If the brain is unable to form images or relate new ideas to those stored in memory, the reader can't understand or remember the new concepts. So other types of reading disabilities can appear when the focus of reading shifts from word identification to comprehension.

Writing, too, involves several brain areas and functions. The brain's networks for vocabulary, grammar, hand movement, and memory must all be in good working order. A developmental writing disorder may result from problems in any of these areas. Someone who can't distinguish the sequence of sounds in a word often has problems with spelling. A person with writing disabilities, particularly expressive language disorders (the inability to express oneself using accurate language or sentence structure), is often unable to compose complete, grammatical sentences.

A student with a developmental arithmetic disorder has trouble recognizing numbers and symbols. Difficulties with memorizing facts such as the multiplication table, aligning numbers, and understanding abstract concepts such as place value and fractions also are symptomatic of a developmental arithmetic disorder.

Another common type of learning disability is an attention disorder. Some students who have attention disorders appear to daydream excessively. Once you get their attention, they may be easily distracted. Individuals with either attention deficit disorder (ADD) or attention deficit hyperactivity disorder (ADHD) often have trouble organizing tasks or completing their work. They don't seem to listen to or follow directions. Their work may be messy and appear careless. Attention disorders, with or without hyperactivity, are not considered learning disabilities in themselves.

Successful celebrities can also have learning disabilities.

© Mitchell Gerber/Corbis

However, because attention problems can seriously interfere with academic performance, they often accompany academic skills disorders.

Here are some additional signs that will help you determine whether you or someone you know has a learning disability:

- Do you perform poorly on tests even when you feel you have studied and are capable of performing better?
- Do you have trouble spelling words?
- Do you work harder than your classmates at basic reading and writing?
- Do your professors tell you that your performance in your courses is "inconsistent"? For example, do you answer questions correctly in class but have trouble writing your answers?
- Do you have a really short attention span, or do your instructors or the people you live with say that you do things "without thinking"?

Responding "yes" to any of the above questions does not necessarily mean that you have a learning disability. But if you are concerned, you can use the resources of your campus's learning center, office of special needs, or student disabilities office to help you deal with any problem you might have and devise ways to learn more effectively.

Anyone who is diagnosed with a learning disability is in good company. Magic Johnson, Jay Leno, Whoopi Goldberg, Tom Cruise, Cher, and Danny Glover are just a few of the famous and successful people with diagnosed learning disabilities.

A final word: A learning disability is a learning difference and is in no way related to intelligence. Having a learning disability is not a sign that you are "dumb." Some of the most intelligent individuals in human history have had learning disabilities.

Where to Go for Help: Learning Styles and Learning Disabilities

On Campus

To learn more about learning styles and learning disabilities, talk to your first-year seminar instructor about campus resources. Most campuses have a learning center and a center for students with learning disabilities. You also may have professors in the areas of education and psychology who have a strong interest in the processes of learning. Finally, don't forget your library or the Internet. A great deal of published information is available to describe how we learn.

Books

Learning Outside the Lines: Two Ivy League Students with Learning Disabilities and ADHD Give You the Tools for Academic Success and Educational Revolution, by Edward M. Hallowell (Foreword), Jonathan Mooney, and David Cole. New York: Fireside, 2000.

Survival Guide for College Students with ADD or LD, by Kathleen G. Nadeau. Washington, DC: Magination Press, 1994.

ADD and the College Student: A Guide for High School and College Students with Attention Deficit Disorder, by Patricia O. Quinn, MD, ed. Washington, DC: Magination Press, 2001.

Online

LD Pride: http://www.ldpride.net/learningstyles.MI.htm. This site was developed in 1998 by Liz Bogod, an adult with learning disabilities. It provides general information about learning styles and learning disabilities and offers an interactive diagnostic tool to determine your learning style.

Support 4 Learning: http://www.support4learning.org .uk/education/learning_styles.cfm. This site is supported by HERO, Higher Education and Research Opportunities, which is the official online gateway to UK universities, colleges, and research organizations. The site provides learning styles inventories and helpful hints about how to use your learning style to do well in college courses.

National Center for Learning Disabilities: http://www.ncld .org. This is the official website for the National Center for Learning Disabilities. The site provides a variety of resources for diagnosing and understanding learning disabilities.

WIRED WINDOW

IF YOU SCORED as having an aural, visual, or read/write preference on the VARK, you can use technology to enhance how you learn course material. Students with an aural preference can use a digital recorder or microcassette recorder to record lectures and then listen to them again later. If you have an iPod, you can purchase a microphone attachment that allows you to use it as a digital audio recorder. Make sure that you have your professors' permission to record their lectures. In addition to recording lectures, you can find supplemental course material through podcasts and via iTunes. A number of colleges and universities provide podcasts for many of their courses free on iTunes. You can browse through course offerings in the iTunesU section or you can search for a term in the iTunes store and limit it to iTunesU results. Try searching the web to find podcasts and audio files to help you enhance your knowledge of a certain topic. (Hint: Try searching for a specific subject and the word "podcast." For instance, you might search "Introduction to Philosophy podcast.") Once you have found the podcasts, you can download the ones that will supplement materials for your course. As with other digital files, create a filing system allows you to find them easily on your iPod or your computer when you need to review the material again later.

Learn

▶▶▶ BUILDING YOUR PORTFOLIO

Are We on the Same Page?

It is what we think we know already that often prevents us from learning.

−Claude Bernard (1813–1878), French physiologist

Complete the VARK (Visual, Aural, Read/Write, and Kinesthetic) Learning Styles Questionnaire in this Step and record your scores here.

Using the guidelines in the textbook, do you have a strong or weak learning preference, or are you multi-modal?

My Vark Scores
Responses marked letter a = _____ (Visual)
Responses marked letter b = _____ (Aural)
Responses marked letter c = _____ (Read/Write)
Responses marked letter d = _____ (Kinesthetic)

Now that you know more about your learning preferences, create a new entry in your portfolio with the title "My VARK Scores." For this entry, write yourself a brief letter to revisit as you begin your second term of college. In this letter, reflect on what you recognize to be your learning preferences and areas that you would like to improve. Be specific in noting the goals you have for using or adapting your learning styles to make the most of your academic experience. Encourage yourself to begin the new term with an open mind and confidence that you can adapt to many different types of learning environments.

Communicating Clearly:

Writing and Speaking for Success

Many people can write, but few can write really well. The same is true of speaking: Some people can speak with authority, while others seem embarrassingly inept.

The ability to write and speak clearly, persuasively, and confidently makes a tremendous difference in how the rest of the world perceives you and how well you will communicate throughout your life. In almost every conceivable occupation, you will be expected

What is this speaker doing to communicate effectively?

© Vince Bucci/Getty Images

to think, create, manage, lead—and communicate. That means you will have to write and speak well. In order to participate in the information age, you will need to be both a good thinker and an excellent communicator.

Most people look at writing and speaking as tasks to be mastered and then forgotten about. Nothing could be farther from the truth. Writing is both a process (a step-by-step method for reaching your final goal) and a product (a final paper, answers to an essay exam, or a script). Similarly, speaking is a skill that involves the mastery of several basic steps. ∎

- that writing is a process leading to a product
- how to use reviews and revisions to strengthen your writing
- why writing email is not the same as writing a college paper
- how best to use your body language and voice when speaking in public
- how to sound organized and composed when speaking on the spot
- what six steps you can take to ensure success in preparing a speech

How Do You Measure Up?

Communicating Clearly

Check the following items that apply to you:

_____ 1. I understand that spoken English, "email English," and formal written English are very different from each other.

_____ 2. I need to spend more than just one night working on a paper if I expect to earn a good grade.

_____ 3. I know that to become a skilled writer, I need to practice my writing.

_____ 4. When preparing to write a paper, I should build in time to collect the information I need before I begin to write.

_____ 5. I know that writing a good paper usually requires many revisions.

_____ 6. I know that the more I narrow a topic for a paper, the easier it is to come up with good ideas.

_____ 7. The best way for me to feel comfortable giving a presentation is to make sure that I know the material well.

_____ 8. Before giving a speech, I always practice what I'm going to say.

_____ 9. When I'm asked an on-the-spot question, I don't panic. I either provide an answer or acknowledge that I don't know the answer.

_____ 10. Although I know how to use a variety of visual aids when giving a speech, I understand that the best visuals in the world can't make up for poor preparation or delivery.

Review the items you did not check. Paying attention to all these aspects of your college experience can be very important to your success. After reading this step, come back to this list and choose an item or two that you did not check but are willing to work on.

Constance Staley, University of Colorado at Colorado Springs, and R. Stephen Staley, Colorado Technical University contributed their valuable and considerable expertise to the section on speaking.

Understanding the Basics of Writing

Few of us—even professionally published writers—say what we want to say, how we want to say it, on our first try at writing it down. But through an understanding of the writing process, practice, and more practice, you can learn to communicate your messages clearly and in the way you want.

The Exploratory/Explanatory Process

Exploratory writing helps you discover what you want to say; explanatory writing then allows you to transmit those ideas to others.

It is important that most or all of your exploratory writing be private, to be read only by you as a series of steps toward your finished work. Keeping your early drafts under wraps frees you to say what you mean and to mean what you say. Later, you will come back and make some adjustments, and each revision will strengthen your message. In contrast, explanatory writing is "published," meaning you have chosen to allow others (your professor, your friends, other students, the public at large) to read it.

Some writers say they gather their best thoughts through exploratory writing—by researching their topics, writing down ideas from their research, and adding their questions and reactions to what they have gathered. As they write, their minds begin to make connections between ideas. They don't attempt to organize, to find exactly the right words, or to think about structure. That might interrupt the thoughts that flow onto the paper or computer screen. They frequently get impatient with themselves for not being able to find the right words. But when they move from exploratory to explanatory writing, their preparation will help them form clear sentences, spell properly, and have their thoughts organized so that their material flows naturally from one point to the next.

© Buddy Mays/CORBIS

The Power of Writing

William Zinsser, author of several books on writing, says, "The act of writing gives the teacher a window into the mind of the student."[1] In other words, your

---

[1]William Zinsser, *On Writing Well* (New York: Harper Resource 25th Anniversary Edition, 2001).

writing provides evidence of how well you think and how well you understand concepts related to your courses. Your writing might also reveal a good sense of humor, a compassion for the less fortunate, a respect for family, and many other things.

Zinsser reminds us that writing is not merely something that writers do but a basic skill for getting through life. He argues that far too many Americans are prevented from doing useful work because they never learned to express themselves. Some people seem to respect actors—who are masters of expression—more than they do writers, but they should consider that writers came up with the words that actors speak.

Finding a Topic

In the book, *Zen and the Art of Motorcycle Maintenance*, Robert Pirsig tells a story about teaching a first-year English class. Each week the assignment was to turn in a 500-word essay. One week, a student failed to submit her paper about the town where the college was located, explaining that she had "thought and thought, but couldn't think of anything to write about." Pirsig gave her an additional weekend to complete the assignment. As he was offering the extension, an idea flashed through his mind. "I want you to write a 500-word paper just about Main Street, not the whole town," he said.

The student stared at him angrily. How was she to narrow her thinking to just one street when she couldn't think of a single thing to write about the entire town? Monday she arrived in tears, sputtering, "I'll never learn to write." Pirsig's response: "Write a paper about one building on Main Street. The opera house. And start with the first brick on the lower left side. I want it by the next class." The student's eyes opened wide. She walked into class the next time with a 5,000-

word paper on the opera house. "I don't know what happened," she exclaimed. "I sat across the street and wrote about the first brick, then the second, and all of a sudden I couldn't stop."[2]

What had Pirsig done for this frustrated student? He had helped her find a focus, a place to begin. And getting started is the biggest writing hurdle most students face. Had this student continued to write about bricks? Of course not. Faced with an ultimatum, she probably began to see for the first time the beauty of the opera house and had gone on to describe it, to find out more about it in the library, to ask others about it, and to comment on its setting among the other buildings on the block.

> **"** *The act of writing gives the teacher a window into the mind of the student.* **"**

TRY IT! The Power of Focused Observation

Think about Pirsig's student who began with the first brick of the opera house and went on to write a 5,000-word paper. Find a favorite spot of yours on campus where you can sit comfortably and undisturbed. Take a good look at the entire area. Now look again, this time noticing specific parts of the area. Choose something: It might be a statue, a building, a tree, or a fence. Now look carefully at just one portion of the object you selected and start writing about it. See where the writing takes you.

---

[2]Robert Pirsig, *Zen and the Art of Motorcycle Maintenance* (New York: Bantam Books, 1984).

Taking the Steps to Better Writing: Prewriting, Writing, and Reviewing

Most writing instructors agree that the writing process consists of these three steps:

1. *Prewriting or rehearsing.* This step includes preparing to write by opening your mind and collecting information from a variety of sources. It also involves recording the information and answers you'll need to track down before you begin. It is generally considered the first stage of exploratory writing.

2. *Writing or drafting.* This is the stage when exploratory writing becomes a rough explanatory draft.

3. *Rewriting or revision.* This is the step when you polish your work until you consider it ready for your public.

Many students skip the first and last steps and "make do" with the middle one. Perhaps the issue is a lack of time or that the student has procrastinated until the night before the paper is due. Whatever the reason, the result is often a poorly written assignment.

Prewriting: The Idea Stage

Many writing experts, among them Donald Murray, believe that of all the steps, prewriting should take the longest.[3] Prewriting is the stage when you write down all you think you need to know about a topic and then go digging for the answers. You might question things that seem illogical. You might recall what you've heard others say. This process of recollecting may lead you to write more and to ask yourself whether your views are more reliable than those of others, whether the topic may be too broad or too narrow, and so forth.

When is a topic appropriate? When is it neither too broad nor too narrow? Test your topic by writing, "The purpose of this paper is to convince my readers

that . . ." (but don't use that stilted phrasing in your paper). Pay attention to the assignment. Know the limits of your knowledge, the limitations on your time, and your ability to do enough research.

Writing: The Drafting and Organizing Stage

Once you have completed your research and feel you have exhausted all information sources and ideas, it's time to move to the writing, or drafting, stage. It is a good idea to begin with an outline so that you can put things where they logically belong, build your paper around a coherent topic, and begin paying attention to the flow of ideas from one sentence to the next and from one paragraph to the next, including subheadings where needed. When you have completed this stage, you will have the first draft of your paper in hand.

Rewriting: The Polishing Stage

Are you finished? Not by a long shot. You have reached the rewriting stage, where you take a good piece of writing and potentially make it great. The essence of good writing is rewriting. You read. You correct. You add smooth transitions. You slash through wordy sentences and delete paragraphs that add nothing to your paper. You substitute strong words for weak ones; sharper vocabulary for fuzzy language. You double-check spelling and grammar. Perhaps you share your work with others who give you feedback. You continue to revise until you're satisfied. You work hard to stay on deadline. And then you "publish."

Allocating Time for Each Writing Stage

When Donald Murray was asked how long a writer should spend on each of the three stages, he offered this breakdown:

- prewriting: 85 percent (including research, thinking, and planning)

[3]Donald Murray, *Learning by Teaching: Selected Articles on Writing and Teaching* (Portsmouth, NH: Boynton/Cook, 1982).

Clearly

It's important to know the "dos" and "don'ts" of email and instant messaging.

- writing: 1 percent (the first draft)
- rewriting: 14 percent (revising until it's right)[4]

If the figures surprise you, here's a true story about a writer who was assigned to create a brochure. He had other jobs to do and kept postponing the work on the brochure. But his other assignments had a direct bearing on the brochure. So even though it appeared that he was putting off the brochure assignment, he was actually researching material for it as he worked on the other projects.

After nearly three months, he sat at his computer and dashed the words off in just under thirty minutes. He felt a rush of ideas, he used words and phrases he'd never used before, and he was afraid to stop until he'd finished. He revised, sent his draft around the office, took some suggestions, and eventually the brochure was published. This writer had spent a long time prewriting (working with related information without trying to write the brochure). He went through the writing stage quickly because his mind was primed for the task. As a result, he had time to polish his work before deciding the job was done.

Mastering Email: Another Method of Communication

Whether we're using a desktop computer or the keypad of a mobile phone, many of us are taking more and more shortcuts with standard English when we compose email and instant messages. Some email writers use no capital letters. Others use little if any punctuation. In her book *Eats, Shoots & Leaves,* Lynne Truss compares today's email shortcuts—such as "C U later"—with the communication style of the child Pip in Charles Dickens's novel Great Expectations, "Mi deer jo I ope u r krwite well."[5]

In some ways, email and instant messaging are a mix of conversational and standard English. Therefore, like conversational English, such communication tends to be more casual than writing on paper. This informality is not always bad. It doesn't make sense to slave over a message for a long time, making sure that your spelling and grammar are perfect and your words are eloquent, if the point of the message is to tell your co-worker that you are ready to go to lunch. But you need to be aware of when it's okay to be casual and breezy and when you have to be formal and meticulous.

An important aspect of electronic mail is that it does not convey emotions nearly as well as face-to-face, or even telephone, conversations. What's missing is tone—the vocal inflection, gestures, and a shared environment that convey what you mean in a regular conversation. Your reader may have difficulty telling if you are serious or kidding, happy or sad, frustrated or fulfilled. Sarcasm is particularly dangerous to use in electronic communications, because it is often missed or misunderstood.[6] Thus, your email compositions will be different from both your paper compositions and your speech.

Further Observations on Becoming a Better Writer and Thinker

Most important, start writing the day you get the assignment, even if it's for only ten or fifteen minutes. That way, you won't be confronting a blank paper as the due date looms. Write something every day, because the more you write, the better you'll write. Cast the net wide for ideas. Reject nothing at first; organize and narrow your thoughts later. Read good writing; it will help you find your own writing style. Above all, know that becoming a better thinker and writer takes hard work, but practice—in this case—can make near-perfect.

[4]Ibid.

[5]Lynne Truss, *Eats, Shoots & Leaves: The Zero Tolerance Approach to Punctuation* (New York: Gotham Books, 2003).
[6]Kaitlin Duck Sherwood, "A Beginner's Guide to Effective Email," **http://www.webfoot.com/advice/email.top.html**.

Becoming a Better Public Speaker

If the biggest writing problem for students is writer's block, then the biggest problem associated with speaking in front of others is fear. Many people dread having to carry out assignments in public speaking. But speaking in front of others doesn't have to be so frightening. When you face such assignments, keep the following thoughts in mind:

- Once you begin speaking, your anxiety is likely to decrease. Anxiety is highest just before or during the first seconds of a presentation.
- Your listeners will generally be unaware of your anxiety. Although your heart sounds as if it is pounding audibly and your knees feel as if they are knocking visibly, these self-perceptions are almost always exaggerated.
- Some anxiety is beneficial. Anxiety indicates that your presentation is important to you. Channel your nervousness into positive energy, and use it to carry yourself enthusiastically and confidently through your talk.
- Practice is the best prevention. The optimal way to reduce your fears is to prepare and rehearse thoroughly. World-famous violinist Isaac Stern is reported to have said, "I practice eight hours a day for forty years, and they call me a genius?!"

Using Body Language and Your Voice

Let your hands hang comfortably at your sides, reserving them for natural, spontaneous gestures. Don't lean over or hide behind the lectern. Unless you must stay close to a fixed microphone, move comfortably about the room, without pacing nervously. Some experts suggest changing physical positions between major points in order to punctuate your presentation. The unconscious message is, "I've finished with that point; let's shift topics." Face your audience, and move toward them while you're speaking.

Here are additional tips for successful speaking:

- Make eye contact with as many listeners as you can. Connecting with your audience in this way helps you read their reactions, demonstrate confidence, and establish command.
- A smile warms up your listeners, although you should avoid smiling excessively or inappropriately. Smiling through a presentation on world hunger would send your listeners a mixed message.

© Barbara Stitzer/PhotoEdit

A relaxed demeanor, eye contact, and appropriate dress are important keys to successful public speaking.

Clearly

- As you practice, pay attention to the pitch of your voice, your rate of speech, and your volume. Project confidence and enthusiasm by varying your pitch. Speak at a rate that mirrors normal conversation—not too fast and not too slow. Consider varying your volume for the same reasons you vary pitch and rate—to engage your listeners and to emphasize important points.

- Be aware of pronunciation and word choice. A poorly articulated word (such as "gonna" for "going to"), a mispronounced word ("nuculer" for "nuclear") or a misused word ("anecdote" for "antidote") can quickly erode credibility. Check meanings and pronunciations in the dictionary if you're not sure of them, and use a thesaurus for word variety. Fillers such as "um," "uh," "like," and "you know" are distracting and detract from the quality of your presentation.

- Consider your appearance. Convey a look of competence, preparedness, and success by dressing professionally.

Speaking on the Spot

Most of the speaking you will do in college, on the job, and in other aspects of life will be extemporaneous or "on the spot"—it will allow for little or no preparation on your part. When your instructor asks your opinion on last night's reading, or when your best friend asks you to defend your views, you have to give impromptu speeches.

When you must speak on the spot, it helps to use a framework that allows you to sound organized and competent. Suppose your instructor asks, "Do you think the world's governments are working together effectively toward establishing a clean global environment?" One of the most popular ways to arrange your thoughts is through the PREP formula. This plan requires the following:

Point of view. Provide an overview—a clear, direct statement or generalization: "After listening to yesterday's lecture, yes, I believe governments are trying to clean up the environment."

Reasons. Broadly state why you hold this point of view: "I was surprised at the efforts of the United Nations General Assembly to focus on the environment."

Evidence or examples. Present specific facts or data supporting your point of view: "For example, the industrialized nations have set stringent goals on air pollution and greenhouse gases for the year 2010."

Point of view restated. To make sure you are understood clearly, end with a restatement of your position: "So, yes, the world's governments seem to be concerned and working to improve the situation."[7]

---

7. Kenneth Wydro, *Think on Your Feet* (Englewood Cliffs, NJ: Prentice-Hall, 1981).

Where to Go for Help: Writing and Speaking

On Campus

Writing center: Most campuses have a writing center—frequently, in the English Department.

Learning assistance center: Learning centers offer assistance with a wide range of learning issues, including help with writing.

Departments of speech, theater, and communications: These departments offer resources and specific courses to help develop speaking skills.

Student activities: One of the best ways to learn and practice speaking skills is to become active in student organizations, especially those such as your student government association and debate club.

Online

Toastmasters International: http://www.toastmasters.org. Click on "10 Tips for Successful Public Speaking."

Six Steps to Better Public Speaking

Successful speaking involves six fundamental steps:

Step 1: Clarify your objective.

Step 2: Analyze your audience.

Step 3: Collect and organize your information.

Step 4: Choose your visual aids.

Step 5: Prepare your notes.

Step 6: Practice your delivery.

Step 1: Clarify Your Objective

Begin by identifying and clarifying what you want to accomplish. Is your goal to inform your listeners about the student government's accomplishments? Or, as a commuting student, do you want to persuade your listeners that your campus needs additional student parking? What do you want your listeners to know, believe, or do when you are finished?

Step 2: Analyze Your Audience

Understand the people you'll be talking to. Ask yourself:

- What do they already know about my topic? If you're going to give a presentation on the health risks of fast food, you'll want to determine how much your listeners already know about fast food so you won't bore them or waste their time.
- What do they want or need to know? How much interest do your classmates have in nutrition? Would they be more interested in some other aspect of college life?
- Who are my listeners? What do they have in common with me?

- What are the audience's attitudes toward me, my ideas, and my topic? How are my listeners likely to feel about the ideas I am presenting? What attitudes have they cultivated about fast food?

Step 3: Collect and Organize Your Information

Now comes the critical part of the process: building your presentation by selecting and arranging blocks of information. A useful analogy is to think of yourself as guiding your listeners through the maze of ideas they already have, so that they gain the new knowledge, attitudes, and beliefs you would like them to have.

© Robert Daly/Getty Images

Imagine your audience. What do they already know about my topic? What do I need to tell them?

Step 4: Choose Your Visual Aids

When visual aids are added to presentations, listeners can absorb 35 percent more information—and over time they can recall 55 percent more. You may choose to prepare a chart, show a video clip, write on the board, or distribute handouts. You may also use your computer to prepare overhead transparencies or dynamic PowerPoint presentations. As you select and use your visual aids, consider these rules of thumb:

- Make visuals easy to follow. Use readable lettering and don't crowd information.
- Explain each visual clearly.
- Allow your listeners enough time to process visuals.
- Proofread carefully. Misspelled words hurt your credibility as a speaker.
- Maintain eye contact with your listeners while you discuss visuals. Don't turn around and address the screen.

Even a state-of-the-art PowerPoint slideshow can't make up for inadequate preparation or poor delivery. But using quality visual aids can help you to organize your material and can help your listeners to understand your message. The quality of your visual aids and your skill in using them can contribute significantly to the overall effectiveness of your presentation.

Step 5: Prepare Your Notes

If you are like most speakers, having an entire written copy of your speech before you may be an irresistible temptation to read much of your presentation. A speech that is read word-for-word will often sound canned or artificial. A better strategy is to memorize only the introduction and conclusion and then use a minimal outline, carefully prepared, from which you can speak extemporaneously. You will rehearse thoroughly in advance. But because you are speaking from brief notes, your choice of words will be slightly different each time you give your presentation, with the result that you will sound prepared but natural. Since you're not reading, you also will be able to maintain eye contact and build rapport with your listeners. You may wish to use note cards because they are unobtrusive. (Make sure you number them, in case you accidentally drop the stack on your way to the front of the room.) After you become more experienced, you may want to let your visuals serve as notes. A handout or PowerPoint slide listing key points may also serve as your basic outline. Eventually, you may find you no longer need notes.

Step 6: Practice Your Delivery

As you rehearse, form a mental image of success rather than failure. Practice your presentation aloud several times to harness that energy-producing anxiety. Begin a few days before your target date, and continue until you're about to go on stage. Make sure you rehearse aloud, as thinking through your speech and talking through your speech have very different results. Practice before an audience—your roommate, a friend, your dog, even the mirror. Talking to someone or something helps simulate the distraction that listeners cause. Consider audiotaping or videotaping yourself to pinpoint your mistakes and to reinforce your strengths. If you ask your practice audience to critique you, you'll have some idea of what changes you might make.

TRY IT!

Presenting Yourself Through PowerPoint

Outline what you would include if you had to prepare a three- to five-slide PowerPoint presentation to introduce yourself to your class. You could create slides about your hobbies, your job, your family, world issues about which you feel passionately, and much more. Plan to include both visuals and text, and make a note of which PowerPoint features you would use to make your presentation as dynamic as possible.

Clearly

WIRED WINDOW

WIKIPEDIA IS AN online encyclopedia that obtains content from its users. You might have used Wikipedia to do research for term papers in high school. Unlike traditional encyclopedias, the content found on Wikipedia is never systematically reviewed by topic experts. So, who can add or edit content on Wikipedia? The answer is *anyone*. Sometimes, this can create chaos on Wikipedia pages when users spend a lot of time quarrelling over facts. Theoretically, these discussions can lead to better content on the more popular Wikipedia pages; however, on less popular pages, information can be grossly inaccurate. Knowing this, it should be no surprise that many of your professors will not allow the use of Wikipedia as a source for your research papers. The discussion of using Wikipedia as a legitimate source continues in the academic world with many faculty members at one extreme of the debate arguing that Wikipedia is nothing more than an opinion-based website, while those on the other end argue that Wikipedia is the ultimate form of peer review. The main point of the argument is that Wikipedia arrives at knowledge by bypassing the established process of scientific inquiry, which includes conducting research that meets certain criteria and publishing that research in periodicals that are reviewed by experts in the field (also referred to as "peer review"). So, before you begin your research papers, check with your professors to see if they will allow you to use Wikipedia as a reference and if they do, use Wikipedia sparingly.

Clearly

▶▶▶ BUILDING YOUR PORTFOLIO

In The Public Eye

According to most studies, people's number one fear is public speaking.
Number two is death. Does that sound right? This means to the average person,
if you go to a funeral, you're better off in the casket than doing the eulogy.

–Jerry Seinfeld (b. 1954), American actor and comedian

The media provide ample opportunities for celebrities and public figures to show off their public speaking skills. As you've probably noticed, some celebrities are much better speakers than others! However, being a good public speaker is not just important for those in the public eye. Whether you want to be a movie star or a marine biologist, potential employers tend to put excellent communication skills at the top of their list of important abilities for job applicants.

1. Create a new entry in your portfolio with the title "In the Public Eye." Record your work for this activity there.

2. Identify a public figure (e.g., David Letterman or Oprah) who, in your opinion, is a good public speaker, and explain why it is important for that person to speak well.

3. List the specific qualities (e.g., humor, eye contact) that you think make that person a good public speaker.

4. Remember the last time you gave a presentation in front of a group, and, using a scale of 1-5 (five being excellent), rate yourself as a public speaker using the guidelines below:

Public Speaking Skills	1 Poor	2 Fair	3 Average	4 Good	5 Excellent
Level of Preparedness (well prepared and confident, last minute technology check)					
Professional Appearance (appropriate business attire, including shoes)					
Effective Vocal Presentation Style (clear and persuasive; good pitch of your voice, rate of speech, and volume; correct grammar)					
Appropriate Behavior and Speech (no chewing gum; avoided fillers such as "um," "uh," "like," and "you know")					
Natural Body Language (good eye contact with audience, appropriate facial expressions, relaxed posture)					
Note your lowest scores: those are areas you probably need to work on as you prepare for your next presentation.					

Listening, Note-Taking, and Participating in Class:

Committing to Classroom Success

In every college class you take, you'll need to master two skills to earn high grades: listening and note-taking. By taking an active role in your classes—genuinely participating by asking questions, contributing to discussions, and providing answers—you will listen better and take more meaningful notes. The reward for your efforts will be an enhanced ability to understand abstract ideas, find new possibilities, organize those ideas, and recall the material once the class is over. This increased capacity to analyze and understand complex material will result in better academic performance while you are in college and also will be valued by a wide range of employers.

© Stock 48/Getty Images

Taking part in class is linked to better listening and note-taking—and ultimately, to better learning.

This step provides valuable suggestions for becoming a skilled listener, note-taker, and class participant. Decide which techniques work best for you. Practice them regularly until they become part of your study routine. ■

In this step you will learn:

- how to listen critically to lectures and class discussion
- how to assess and improve your note-taking skills
- how good class notes can help you do your homework
- how to prepare before class
- why it's important to review your notes soon after class
- how to review class and textbook materials after class
- how to take notes in math and science courses
- why you should speak up in class

How Do You Measure Up?

Listening, Note-Taking, and Participating in Class

Check the following items that apply to you:

____ 1. I always do the assigned reading in preparation for my classes.

____ 2. When I arrive at class early, I spend the time before class reviewing the reading assignment or my notes from the previous lecture.

____ 3. If the instructor puts an outline on the board or on a PowerPoint slide, I copy each part as we come to it in the lecture.

____ 4. During the lecture I try to determine what information is most important.

____ 5. During class I write down all key points in my notes.

____ 6. If I realize that I have missed something important in my notes, I ask the professor or a classmate for the information.

____ 7. If I do not understand something, I do not hesitate to ask questions in class, even in large lecture sections.

____ 8. I take notes on class discussions as well as on lectures.

____ 9. When I have to miss class, I contact the instructor immediately—if possible, before class begins.

____ 10. I belong to a study group for one or more of my classes, and we meet often to go over our notes and prepare for exams.

Review the items you did not check. Paying attention to all these aspects of your college experience can be very important to your success. After reading this step, come back to this list and choose an item or two that you did not check but are willing to work on.

Jeanne L. Higbee of the University of Minnesota, Twin Cities contributed her valuable and considerable expertise to the writing of this section.

Knowing the Basics of Listening and Note-Taking

Listening and note-taking are critical to your academic success because your professors are likely to introduce material in class that your texts don't cover. Chances are good that much of this material will resurface on quizzes and exams.

Here are tips for ensuring that you will retain what is important from class:

- Instead of chatting with friends before class, review your study notes for the previous class.
- If you would like to record a lecture, request the instructor's permission first. Also consider asking the instructor to speak slowly or to repeat key points. And even if you're recording, take notes, too.
- Be aware that what the instructor says in a lecture may not always be in the textbook and vice versa. Also consider that an instructor often thinks that what she says in class is more important than what the text says, and that you are therefore more likely to see class material on a test.
- Because writing down everything the instructor says is impossible, and you may be unsure that you have recorded everything that is important, ask questions in class (or after class if your professor prefers). The instructor is always the best source, and this practice will ensure that you more clearly understand your notes. Going over your notes with someone from your campus learning center or comparing your notes with your study team's or a friend's notes may also help you.
- Take notes on the class discussion as well as the lecture. Your professor may be taking notes on what is said in discussion and could use the information in exams.

While you are taking notes, also be sure to participate in class discussion. Whether you're in class or in another situation, you will tend to remember what you have said more than what others are saying to you.

Note-Taking Systems

You can make the best use of your class time by using your listening skills to take effective notes. But first, you have to decide on a system.

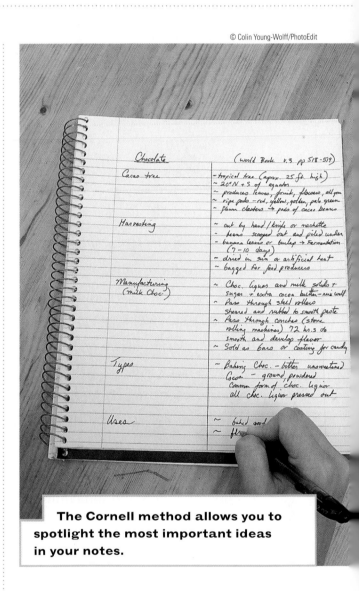

© Colin Young-Wolff/PhotoEdit

The Cornell method allows you to spotlight the most important ideas in your notes.

Cornell Format In the Cornell format you create a "recall" column on each page of your notebook by drawing a vertical line a few inches from the left border.

Outline Format The outline format represents key ideas by Roman numerals, and other ideas relating to each key idea by uppercase letters, numbers, and lowercase letters.

Paragraph Format The paragraph format involves writing detailed paragraphs, with each containing a summary of a topic.

List Format The list format can be effective when taking notes on terms and definitions, sequences, or facts.

Once you have decided on a format for taking notes, you may also want to develop your own system of abbreviations. For example, you might write "inst" instead of "institution" or "eval" instead of "evaluation." Just make sure you will be able to understand your abbreviations when it's time to review.

Note-Taking Techniques

Once you've decided on a note-taking system, use these techniques to put that system to work.

1. Identify the main ideas. Well-organized lectures always contain key points. The first principle of effective note-taking is to write down these main ideas around which the lecture is built. Although supporting details are important as well, focus your note-taking on the main ideas.

Some instructors announce the purpose of a lecture or offer an outline, thus providing the class with the skeleton of main ideas, followed by the details. Others develop overhead transparencies or PowerPoint presentations and may make these materials available on a class website before the lecture.

2. Don't try to write down everything. Attempting to record every word from a class lecture or discussion will distract you from an essential activity: thinking. If you're an active listener, you will ultimately have shorter but more useful notes.

3. Don't be thrown by a disorganized lecturer. When a lecturer is disorganized, it's your job to try to organize what she says into general and specific frameworks. When the order is not apparent, indicate in your notes where the gaps lie. After the lecture, consult your reading material, study team, or a classmate to fill in these gaps, or visit the instructor during office hours with your questions.

4. Return to your recall column. As soon after class as feasible, preferably within an hour or two, sift through your notes and use a recall column (the left column in your notes) to write down the main ideas and important details for tests and examinations. For many students, this step is a critical part of effective note-taking and becomes an important study device for test preparation. In anticipation of using your notes later, treat each page of your notes as part of an exam-preparation system.

Class Notes and Homework

Good class notes can help you complete homework assignments, too. Follow these steps.

1. Take ten minutes to review your class notes. Skim the notes and put a question mark next to anything you do not understand at first reading. Draw stars next to topics that are especially important.

2. Do a warm-up for your homework. Before starting the assignment, look through your notes again. Use a separate sheet of paper to rework examples, problems, or exercises. If there is related assigned material in the textbook, review it. Go back to the text examples. Cover the solutions and attempt to answer each question or complete each problem.

3. Do assigned problems and answer assigned questions. When you start your homework, read each question or problem and ask, What am I supposed to find or find out? What is essential and what is extraneous? Read each problem several times and state it in your own words. Work the problem without referring to your notes or the text.

4. Don't give up. When you encounter a problem or question that you cannot readily handle, move on only after a reasonable effort. After you have completed the entire assignment, return to the items that stumped you. Try once more, and then take a break. You may need to mull over a particularly difficult problem for several days.

5. Complete your work. When you finish an assignment, consider what you learned from the exercise. Think about how the problems and questions were different from one another, which strategies you used to solve them, and what form the answers took. Review any material you have not mastered. Ask the professor, a classmate, your study group, someone in the campus learning center, or a tutor to help you with difficult problems and questions.

TRY IT! Try It! Working Together by Comparing Notes

Pair up with another student and compare your class notes for this course. Are your notes clear? Do you agree on what is important? Take a few minutes to explain your note-taking systems to each other. Agree to use a recall column during the next class meeting. Afterward, share your notes again and check on how each of you used the recall column. Again, compare your notes and what each of you deemed important.

Striving for Success Before, During, and After Class

Before Class: Prepare to Remember

Even if lectures don't allow for active participation, you can take a number of active learning steps before your classes to make your listening and note-taking efficient.

1. Do the assigned reading. Unless you do the assigned reading before class, you may not be able to follow the lecture. Some instructors refer to assigned readings for each class session; others may simply provide a syllabus (an overall outline of the course, with assignments and dates) at the start of the course and assume you are keeping up with the assigned readings.

2. Pay attention to your course syllabus. Syllabi are formal statements of course expectations, requirements, and procedures. Many instructors assume that once students have received the syllabus, they will understand and follow course requirements with few or even no reminders.

3. Use additional materials provided by the instructor. Many professors post lecture outlines or notes to a website prior to class. Download and print these materials for easy reference during class. They often provide hints to what the instructor considers most important; they also can create an organizational structure for note-taking.

4. Warm up for class. Before class begins, warm up or "preview" by reviewing chapter introductions and summaries and by referring to related sections in your text. Also review your notes from the previous class period, since that material may be related to, or even necessary to understanding, the upcoming material. Taking this step prepares you to pay attention, understand, and remember once class begins.

5. Keep an open mind. Your classes will expose you to new ideas and different perspectives. Some instructors may present information that challenges your value system. One of the purposes of college is to teach you to think in new and different ways and to learn to feel confident about your own beliefs. Instructors want you to think for yourself, and they do not necessarily expect you to agree with everything they or your classmates say.

Always complete your reading assignments on time.

© Digital Vision/Getty Images

6. Get organized. Develop an organizational system. Decide what type of notebook will work best for you. Many study skills experts suggest using three-ring binders because you can punch holes in syllabi and other course handouts and keep them with class notes. If you prefer using spiral notebooks, consider buying multi-subject notebooks that have pocket dividers for handouts, or create a folder for each course.

7. Prepare to track your progress. Create a recording system to keep track of grades on all assignments, quizzes, and tests. Retain any papers that are returned to you until the term is over and your grades are posted on your transcript. That way, if you need to appeal a grade because an error occurs, you will have the documentation required to support your appeal.

During Class: Listen Critically

Listening in class is not like listening to a TV program, a friend, or even a speaker at a meeting. Knowing how to listen in class can help you recall and understand what you have heard and can save you time. Here are some suggestions.

1. Be ready for the message. Prepare yourself to hear, to listen, and to receive the message. If you have done the assigned reading, you will know what details are already in the text so that you can focus your notes on key concepts during the lecture. You will also know what information is not covered in the text, and you will be prepared to pay especially close attention when the instructor is presenting unfamiliar material.

2. Listen for the main concepts and central ideas, not just facts and figures. Although facts are important, they will be easier to remember and will make more sense when you can place them in a context of themes and ideas. You want to understand the material, and only memorizing facts and figures won't help you understand it.

3. Listen for new ideas. Even if you know a lot about a topic, you can still learn something new. Do not assume that college instructors will present the same information you learned in a similar course in high school.

4. Really hear what is said. Hearing words is not the same as hearing the intended message. Listening involves hearing what the speaker wants you to understand. Don't give in to distractions, and try not to pass quick judgment on what is being said. Make a note of questions that arise in your mind as you listen, but save the judgments for later.

5. Repeat mentally. Words can go in one ear and out the other unless you make an effort to retain them. Think about what you hear and restate it silently in your own words. If you cannot translate the information into your own words, ask for clarification.

6. Decide whether what you have heard is not important, somewhat important, or very important. If a point in the lecture is really not important, let it go. If it's very important, make it a major point in your notes by highlighting or underscoring it. If it's somewhat important, try to relate it to a very important topic by writing it down as a subset of that topic.

7. Ask questions. Early in the term, determine whether the instructor is open to responding to questions during a lecture. Some professors prefer to save questions for the end or to have students ask questions during separate discussion sections or office hours. To some extent, the optimal timing for questions may depend on the nature of the class—that is, whether it is a large lecture or a small seminar.

8. Listen to the entire message. Concentrate on the big picture, but also pay attention to specific details and examples that can assist you in understanding and retaining the information.

9. Respect your own ideas and those of others. You already know a lot of things. Your own thoughts and ideas are valuable, and you should not discard them just because someone else's views conflict with your own. At the same time, you should not reject the ideas of others too casually.

10. Sort, organize, and categorize. When you listen, try to match what you are hearing with what you already know. Take an active role in deciding how best to recall what you are learning.

After Class: Respond, Recite, Review

Most forgetting takes place within the first twenty-four hours after you see or hear something. Don't let the forgetting curve take its toll on you. As soon after class as possible, review your notes and fill in the details you still remember, but missed writing down, in those spaces you left on the right-hand side of the page.

Use these three important steps for remembering the key points in the lecture:

1. Write the main ideas in the recall column next to the material they represent. For five or ten minutes, quickly review your notes and select key words or phrases that will act as labels or tags for main ideas and key information in the notes.

2. Use the recall column to recite your ideas. Cover the notes on the right and use the prompts from the recall column to help you recite out loud a brief version of what you understand from the class in which you have just participated. If you don't have a few minutes after class when you can concentrate on going over your notes, find some other time during that same day to review them.

3. Review previous class notes just before the next class session. As you sit in class waiting for it to begin, use the time to review the notes from the previous class. This preparation will put you in tune with the lecture or discussion that is about to begin and also prompt you to ask questions about material from the previous class period that may not have been clear to you.

These three ways to engage with the material will pay dividends later, when you study for your exams.

Taking Notes in Nonlecture and Quantitative Courses

Nonlecture and quantitative courses—like mathematics, chemistry, or physics—pose special challenges when it comes to note-taking. The following advice and tips will help you hone the skills you've learned in this step to these kinds of courses.

Nonlecture Courses

Be ready to adapt your note-taking methods to match the situation. Group discussion has become a popular way to teach in college because it involves active learning. On your campus you may also have Supplemental Instruction (SI) classes that provide further opportunity to discuss the information presented in lectures. How can you keep a record of what's happening in such classes?

Assume you are taking notes in an in-class problem-solving group assignment. You would begin your notes by asking yourself "What is the problem?" and writing the problem down. As the discussion progresses, you would list the solutions offered. These would be your main ideas. The important details might include the positive and negative aspects of each view or solution. The important thing to remember when taking notes in nonlecture courses is that you need to record the information presented by your classmates as well as by the instructor, and to consider all reasonable ideas, even though they may differ from your own.

Know how to apply what you've learned in this step to taking effective notes in your math and science courses.

How to organize the notes you take in a class discussion depends on the purpose or form of the discussion. But it usually makes good sense to begin with the list of issues or topics that the discussion leader announces. Another approach is to list the questions that the participants raise for discussion. If the discussion is exploring reasons for and against a particular argument, it is reasonable to divide your notes into columns or sections for pros and cons. When conflicting views arise in the discussion, it is important to record the different perspectives and the rationales behind them.

Quantitative Courses

Many quantitative courses such as mathematics, chemistry, and physics often build on each other from term to term and from year to year. When you take notes in these courses, you are likely to need to refer back to them in future terms. For example, when taking organic chemistry, you may need to go back to notes taken in earlier chemistry courses. This review process can be particularly important when time has passed since your last course, such as after a summer break. Here are some ideas for getting organized:

- Keep your notes and supplementary materials (such as instructors' handouts) for each course in a separate three-ring binder labeled with the course number and name.
- Before class, download any notes, outlines, or diagrams, charts, graphs, and other visual representations of the material provided on the instructor's website, and bring them to class. You can save yourself considerable time and distraction during the lecture if you do not have to copy complicated graphs and diagrams while the instructor is talking.
- Take notes only on the front of each piece of loose-leaf paper. Later, you can use the back of each sheet to add further details, annotations, corrections, comments, questions, and a summary of each lecture. Alternatively, once you've placed what have now become the left-hand pages in the binder, you can use them the same way that you would use the recall column in the Cornell format, noting key ideas to be used for testing yourself when preparing for exams.

- Consider taking your notes in pencil or erasable pen. When copying long equations while also trying to pay attention to what the instructor is saying, or when copying problems that students are solving at the board, it is not unusual to need to erase or make changes. You want to keep your notes as neat as possible.
- Organize your notes in your binder chronologically. Then create separate tabbed sections for homework, lab assignments, returned tests, and other materials.
- If the instructor distributes handouts in class, label them and place them in your binder either immediately before or immediately after the notes for that day.
- Keep your binders for math and science courses until you graduate (or even longer if there is any chance that you will attend graduate school in the future). They will serve as beneficial review materials for later classes in math and science sequences and for preparing for standardized tests such as the Graduate Record Exam (GRE) or the Medical College Admission Test (MCAT).

Tips for note-taking in quantitative courses

Taking notes in math and science courses can be different from taking notes for other types of classes, where it may not be a good idea to try to write down every word the instructor says. Here are some tips geared specifically to taking notes in math and science classes:

- Write down any equations, formulas, diagrams, charts, graphs, and definitions that the instructor puts on the board or screen.
- Quote the instructor's words as precisely as possible. Technical terms often have exact meanings and cannot be paraphrased.
- Use standard symbols, abbreviations, and scientific notation.
- Write down all worked problems and examples, step by step. They often provide the format for exam questions. Actively try to solve the problem yourself as it is solved at the front of the class. Be sure that you can follow the logic and understand the sequence of steps.
- Listen carefully to other students' questions and the instructor's answers. Take notes on the discussion and during question-and-answer periods.
- Use asterisks, exclamation points, question marks, or symbols of your own to highlight important points or questions in your notes.
- Refer back to the textbook after class; it may contain more accurate diagrams and other visual representations than you are able to draw while taking notes in class.

Speaking Up in Class

Learning is not a spectator sport. To really learn, you must talk about what you are learning, write about it, relate it to past experiences, and make what you learn part of yourself. Participation is the heart of active learning. When you say something in class, you are more likely to remember it than what someone else says. So when an instructor directs a question your way and you answer it, or when you ask a question, you're actually making it easier to remember the day's lesson.

Some students are reluctant to participate in class. You might have gone to a high school where students who expressed their opinions or asked questions in class were thought of as nerds. Sometimes adult students are afraid that class participation will reveal their lack of knowledge. But in order to get the most out of college classes, you'll need to conquer those feelings and fears and let your voice be heard.

Naturally, you will be more likely to participate in a class where the instructor emphasizes the value of discussion, calls on students by name, shows students signs of approval and interest, and avoids criticizing anyone for an incorrect answer. Often, answers that you and others offer that are not quite correct can lead to new perspectives on a topic.

Unfortunately, large classes often leave instructors little choice but to use the lecture method. And large classes can be intimidating. If you speak up in a class of 100 and think you've made a fool of yourself, you may fear that 99 other people will know it. But that conclusion is somewhat unrealistic, because in many cases you've probably asked a question that others were too timid to ask, and they'll silently be thanking you for making the effort. If you're lucky, you might even find that the instructor in a large class takes time out to ask or answer questions.

To take advantage of the many opportunities for participating actively in all classes, try these techniques:

1. Sit as close to the front as possible. If you're seated by name and your name begins with z, plead bad eyesight or poor hearing—anything to get moved up front.

© Prisma/SuperStock

Don't hesitate to ask your instructor questions during or after class.

tion to the rest of the class. In each case, you benefit in several ways. The instructor gets to know you, other students get to know you, and you learn from both the instructor and your classmates. But don't overdo it. The instructor and your peers will tire of too many questions that disrupt the flow of the class.

5. Speak up in class. Ask a question or volunteer to answer a question or make a comment. It becomes easier every time you do so.

6. Never feel that you're asking a "stupid" question. If you don't understand something, you have a right to ask for an explanation.

7. When the instructor calls on you to answer a question, don't bluff. If you know the answer, give it. If you're not certain, begin with, "I think . . ., but I'm not sure I have it all correct." If you don't know, just say so.

8. If you've recently read a book or an article that is relevant to the class topic, bring it in. Use related outside reading either to ask questions about the material or to provide additional information that was not covered in class.

So the next time you have the opportunity, speak up in class. The time will go by faster, your classmates and instructors will get to know you, and your professors will likely be grateful for your enthusiastic participation.

2. Focus your eyes on the lecturer. Sitting up front will make this easier for you to do.

3. Listen carefully to the lecture. Do not put yourself in a situation where you might be distracted. It might be wise, for example, not to sit near friends, who can be distracting without meaning to be.

4. Raise your hand when you don't understand something. The instructor may answer you immediately, ask you to wait until later in the class, or throw your ques-

Where to Go for Help: Listening, Note-Taking, and Participating in Class

On Campus

Learning assistance center: Almost every campus has one of these, and the skills in this step are among their specialties. More and more, the best students—and good students who want to be the best students—use the campus learning center as often as students who are having academic difficulties. These services are offered by both full-time professionals and highly skilled student tutors who are available at times convenient for you.

Fellow college students: Often the best help you can get is from your fellow students—but of course, not just any students. Keep an eye out in your classes, residence hall, cocurricular groups, and other places for the most serious, purposeful, and directed students. They are the ones to seek out. Find a student tutor. Join a study group. Students who use these readily available peer resources are much more likely to stay in college and succeed. It does not diminish you in any way to seek assistance from your peers.

Online

Mary Helen Callarman Center for Academic Excellence at the University of Central Florida: **http://www.sarc.sdes.ucf.edu/studyhandouts.php**. This excellent web link gives tips on study skills.

Engage

WIRED WINDOW

YOU WILL DISCOVER many options for using technology to enhance your note-taking skills and your engagement with learning. Some students prefer to bring their laptops to class and either type their notes or use the tablet feature to handwrite their notes into digital files. We think it's important to strike a balance between taking notes on your computer and paying attention to class discussion. Most students can't type as quickly as they can write and will need to be much more selective about the information they choose to enter, so you might face a greater challenge extracting the most important points of the lecture or discussion while it is happening. QipIt, a free service, allows you to take pictures of documents including PowerPoint presentations, whiteboard notes, and overheads, and have them converted to digital documents. If you choose to use such a service, make sure you have obtained permission from your professors to reproduce their notes. Whether you use QipIt or type your own notes in a word processor, it's helpful to organize them so you can find what you are looking for. Assign file names that reflect the content of the notes and the date you took them.

▶▶▶ BUILDING YOUR PORTFOLIO

Making Meaning

It is important that students bring a certain ragamuffin, barefoot irreverence to their studies; they are not here to worship what is known, but to question it.

–Jacob Bronowski (1908–1974), English-Polish mathematician

This step includes several examples of note-taking strategies, but did you catch the emphasis on what you do with your notes after class? Sometimes it is helpful to associate a concept with something of interest to you. And often, preparing to teach someone else how to do something or explaining a complex idea to others can help you to fully understand the information.

1. Create a new entry in your portfolio with the title "Making Meaning." Record your work for this activity there.

2. Choose a set of current class notes (it doesn't matter which class) and specifically look for connections between the subject matter and your personal interests and goals (future career, social issue, sports, hobbies, etc.)

   a. Next, develop a five-minute presentation using PowerPoint to present to your classmates; your presentation should outline your class notes and show the connection to your interests.

      i. Introduction slide

         Tip: Be sure to include your name and the date of the presentation.

      ii. Content slides (a good rule of thumb is one slide per minute)

         Tip: Keep your slides simple by focusing on key words and concepts. Use short phrases rather than complete sentences so you won't be tempted to read directly from the slide.

      iii. Closing slides

         Tip: Anticipate questions your audience might have by reviewing the questions at the end of the textbook chapter or by recalling questions that were asked during your class session.

3. Write a brief introduction/description and then attach your PowerPoint presentation to your description. You probably won't be creating PowerPoint presentations for all of your class notes, but making a habit of connecting class content to your life is an easy way of remembering information. When it is time to prepare for a test, try pulling your notes into a presentation that you would feel comfortable presenting to your classmates--after that, the exam should be a breeze!

Reading for Success:

Mastering an Essential Skill

Why is reading college textbooks more challenging than reading high school texts or reading for pleasure? The answer is that college textbooks are loaded with terms, concepts, and complex information that you are expected to learn on your own in a short time. To succeed, you will need to learn, and use, a reading method such as the one described in this step.

A textbook reading plan can pay off. It can increase your focus and concentration, promote greater understanding of what you read, and prepare you to study for tests and exams. This system is based on four main steps: previewing, reading, marking, and reviewing. ■

College courses often require reading beyond the textbook.

In this step you will learn:

- how to prepare to read textbooks
- how to preview reading material
- how to read your textbooks efficiently
- how to mark your textbooks
- how to review your reading
- how to adjust your reading style to the material for courses of various kinds—quantitative, social sciences, and humanities
- how to build your vocabulary

How Do You Measure Up?

Reading for Success

Check the following items that apply to you:

____ 1. I skim or "preview" a chapter before I begin to read.

____ 2. I concentrate while reading a text.

____ 3. I wait to underline, highlight, or annotate the text until after I have read a page or section.

____ 4. I take notes while I read.

____ 5. I pause at the end of each section or page to review what I have read.

____ 6. After reading, I recite key ideas to myself or with a study partner.

____ 7. When reading a textbook, I use a dictionary to check the meaning of unfamiliar words.

____ 8. I know the difference between a textbook and primary source material.

____ 9. I look for connections between the text and class lectures and discussions.

____ 10. I set reading goals for each study period and take a short break when I have reached my goal.

Review the items you did not check. Paying attention to all these aspects of your college experience can be very important to your success. After reading this Step, come back to this list and choose an item or two that you did not check but are willing to work on.

Jeanne L. Higbee of the University of Minnesota, Twin Cities and Mary Ellen O'Leary of the University of South Carolina at Columbia contributed their valuable and considerable expertise to the writing of this section.

Previewing Before You Read

The purpose of previewing is to get the big picture, to understand how what you are about to read is connected to what you already know and to the material the instructor is covering in class. Begin by reading the title of the chapter. Next, quickly read the introductory paragraphs, and then read the summary at the beginning or end of the chapter (if there is a summary). Skim through the chapter headings and subheadings. Finally, note any study exercises at the end of the chapter.

As part of your preview, check the number of pages the chapter contains. Estimate how many pages you can reasonably expect to cover in your first fifty-minute study period.

Different types of textbooks may require more or less time to read. For example, depending on your interests and previous knowledge, you may be able to read a psychology text more quickly than a logic text that presents a whole new system of symbols.

Mapping a Chapter

Mapping a chapter as you preview it provides a visual guide to how the different ideas fit together. Because about 75 percent of students identify themselves as visual learners, mapping is an excellent learning tool.

How do you map a chapter? While you are previewing, draw either a wheel or a branching structure. In the wheel structure, place the central idea of the chapter in the circle. You should find the central idea in the chapter introduction; it may also be apparent in the chapter title. Place secondary ideas on the spokes radiating from the circle, and draw offshoots of those ideas on the lines attached to the spokes. In the branching structure, put the main idea (most likely the title) at the top, followed by supporting ideas on the second tier, and so forth.

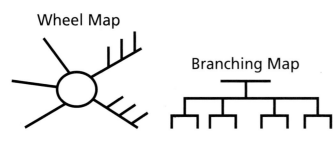

Wheel Map

Branching Map

Wheel maps and branching maps can help you organize information visually and make it easier to remember.

Alternatives to Mapping

Perhaps you prefer a more linear visual image. If so, consider making an outline of the headings and subheadings in the chapter. Another option is to make a list. Creating a list can be particularly effective when you are reading a text that introduces many new terms and their definitions. Divide the terms in your list into groups of five, seven, or nine, and leave white space between the clusters so that you can visualize each group in your mind. This practice is known as "chunking." Research indicates that we learn material better in chunks of five, seven, or nine.

If you are an interactive learner, make a list or create a flash card for each heading and subheading. Then fill in the list or the back of each card after reading the corresponding section in the text. Use your lists or flash cards to review with a partner or to recite the material to yourself.

Previewing, combined with mapping, outlining, listing, or using flash cards, may require more time up front, but it will save you time later because you will have created an excellent review tool for quizzes and tests. You will be using your visual learning skills as you set up "advance organizers" to help you associate details of the chapter with the larger ideas.

As you preview the text material, look for connections between the text and the related lecture material. Call to mind the related terms and concepts that you recorded in the lecture. Use these strategies to warm up. Ask yourself, "Why am I reading this? What do I need to learn?"

Reading Your Textbook

Read before you highlight After previewing, you are ready to read the text. With your skeleton map, outline, or list you should be able to read more quickly and with greater comprehension than you could without these tools. To avoid marking the text too much and marking the wrong information, first read without using your pencil or highlighter. When you have reached the end of a section, ask yourself, "What are the key ideas in this section? What do I think I'll see on the test?" Then and only then, decide what to underline or highlight.

Annotate You may want to try a reading strategy known as annotating. Annotating involves writing the key ideas in the margins of the text, in your own words.

Learn to concentrate Many students have trouble concentrating and not understanding the content when reading textbooks. Many factors may affect your

Read

Taking careful notes and reviewing them with a friend can make your study time more productive.

TRY IT!

Preparing to Read, Think, and Mark

Choose a reading assignment for one of your classes. After previewing the material, begin reading until you reach a major heading or until you have read at least a page or two. Now stop and write down what you remember from the material. Next go back to the same material and mark what you believe are the main ideas. Don't fall into the trap of marking too much. Now list four of the main ideas from the reading:

1. _____

2. _____

3. _____

4. _____

ability to concentrate and understand what you are reading: the time of day, your energy level, your interest in the material, and your study location.

Consider these suggestions, and decide which would help improve your reading ability:

- Find a quiet study location. If you are on campus, the library is your best option.

- Read in fifty-minute blocks of time, with short breaks in between. By reading for fifty minutes frequently during the day instead of cramming in all your reading at the end of the day, you should be able to understand and retain the material more easily.

- Set goals for your study period, such as "I will read twenty pages of my psychology text in the next fifty minutes." Reward yourself with a ten-minute break after each fifty-minute study period.

- If you are having trouble concentrating or staying awake, take a quick walk around the library or down the hall. Then resume studying.

- Jot study questions in the margins, take notes, or recite key ideas. Reread confusing parts of the text, and make a note to ask your instructor for clarification.

- Experiment with your reading rate. Try to move your eyes more quickly over the material by focusing on phrases, not individual words.

- Focus on the important portions of the text. Pay attention to the first and last sentences of paragraphs and to words in italics or bold print.

- If the text has a glossary, consult it for the definition of unfamiliar terms. Use the dictionary if the text doesn't have a glossary.

Use the front matter and end-of-chapter aids As you begin reading, you can learn more about the text-

book and its author by reading the front matter in the book—the preface, foreword, introduction, and author's biographical sketch. The preface, usually written by the author, explains why the book was written and what material is covered.

Many textbooks have a preface written to the instructor and a separate preface for students. The foreword is often an endorsement of the book written by someone other than the author. Some books will have an additional introduction that reviews the book's overall organization and its contents chapter by chapter.

Many textbooks have questions at the end of each chapter that you can use as a study guide or quick check to see if you understand the chapter's main points. Take time to read and respond to these questions, whether or not your instructor requires you to do so.

Understand the purpose of the text Textbooks aim to cover a lot of material in a fairly limited space. But a text won't necessarily tell you everything you want to know about a topic—it may omit things that would make your reading more interesting. If you find yourself fascinated by a particular topic, go to the primary sources—the original research or documents the author used in writing the text.

Because some textbooks are sold with "test banks" to aid faculty in creating quizzes and tests, your instructors may draw their examinations directly from the text. On the other hand, they may consider the textbook to be supplementary to their lectures. When in doubt, ask for a clarification of what will be covered on the test and what types of questions will be used.

Finally, not all textbooks are equal. Some are simply better designed and better written than others. If you find a particular textbook to be disorganized in its physical layout or content, or exceptionally hard to understand, let your instructor know your opinion.

Reading to Question, to Interpret, and to Understand

Monitor Your Comprehension

An important aspect of textbook reading is monitoring your comprehension. As you read, ask yourself, "Do I understand this?" If not, stop and reread the material. Look up words that you don't know. Try to clarify the main points and their relationship to one another.

Another way to check comprehension is to recite the material aloud to yourself, a study partner, or your study group. Using a study partner or group to monitor your comprehension gives you immediate feedback and is highly motivating. One way that study group members can work together is to divide up a chapter for previewing and studying and to get together later to teach the material to one another.

Mark Your Textbook

Marking your textbooks is an active reading strategy that may help you concentrate on the material as you read. In addition, you may use your text notations when studying for tests. You may like to underline, to highlight, or use margin notes or annotations. No matter which method you prefer, remember these two important guidelines:

1. Read before you mark. Finish reading a section before you decide which are the most important ideas and concepts. Mark only those ideas, using your preferred methods (highlighting, underlining, circling key terms, annotating).

2. Think before you mark. When you read a text for the first time, everything may seem important. Only after you have completed a section and reflected on it will you be ready to identify the key ideas. Ask yourself, "What are the most important ideas? What will I see on the test?" This procedure can help you avoid marking too much material.

Two other considerations may affect your decisions about textbook marking. First, if you just make notes or underline directly on the pages of your textbook, you are committing yourself to at least one more viewing of all the pages that you have already read—the entire 400 pages of your anatomy or art history textbook. A more productive use of your time might be taking notes,

creating flash cards, making lists, or outlining textbook chapters. These methods are also more practical if you intend to review with a friend or study group.

Second, sometimes highlighting or underlining can provide you with a false sense of security. You may have determined what information is most important, but you may not necessarily have tested your understanding of the material. When you force yourself to put something in your own words while taking notes, you are not only predicting exam questions but also evaluating whether you can answer them clearly. These active reading strategies take more time initially, but they can save you time in the long run because they promote concentration and make it easy to review—so that you probably won't have to pull an all-nighter before an exam.

Recycle Your Reading: Review and Preview the Key Ideas

After you have read and marked or taken notes on the key ideas from the first section of the chapter, proceed to each subsequent section until you have finished the chapter. After you have completed each section—and before you move on to the next section—ask again, "What are the key ideas? What will I see on the test?" At the end of each section, try to guess what information the author will present in the next section. Good reading should lead you from one section to the next, with each new section adding to your understanding.

Review Daily

The final step in effective textbook reading is reviewing. Many students expect the improbable—that they will read through their text material one time and be able to remember the ideas four, six, or even twelve weeks later at exam time. More realistically, you will need to include regular reviews in your study process. Here is where your notes, study questions, annotations, flash cards, visual maps, or outlines will be most useful. Your study goal should be to review the material from each chapter every week.

Consider ways to use your many senses to review. Recite aloud. Tick off each item in a list on each of your fingertips. Post diagrams, maps, or outlines around your living space so that you will see them often and will likely be able to visualize them while taking the test.

Adjust Your Reading Style

With effort, you can improve your reading dramatically, but remember to be flexible. How you read should depend on the material. Assess the relative importance and difficulty of the assigned reading, and adjust your reading style and the time you allot accordingly. Connect one important idea to another by asking yourself, "Why am I reading this? Where does this fit in?" When the textbook material is virtually identical to the lecture material, you can save time by concentrating mainly on one or the other. It takes planning to read textbooks and other assigned readings with good understanding and recall.

Develop Your Vocabulary

Textbooks are full of new terminology. In fact, one could argue that learning chemistry is largely a matter of learning the language of chemists and that mastering philosophy or history or sociology requires a firm grounding in the terminology of each particular academic discipline or field of study.

If words are such a basic and essential component of our knowledge, what is the best way to learn them? Follow these vocabulary-building strategies:

- During your overview of the chapter, notice and jot down unfamiliar terms. Consider making a flash card for each term or writing the terms in a list.

- When you encounter challenging words, consider the context. See if you can predict the meaning of an unfamiliar term by using the surrounding words.

- If context by itself is not enough, try analyzing the term to discover the root, or base part, or other meaningful parts of the word. For example, "emissary" has a root that means "to emit" or "to send forth," so we can guess that an emissary is someone sent forth with a message. Similarly, note prefixes and suffixes. For example, "anti-" means "against" and "pro-" means "for."

- Use a dictionary or go to **http://www.merriam-webster.com/netdict.htm** (The Merriam-Webster Dictionary online) to find any definition you need. Note any multiple definitions and search for the meaning that fits the usage you are looking for.

> " *With effort, you can improve your reading dramatically, but remember to be flexible.* How you read should depend on the material. "

- Take opportunities to use any new terms you've learned in your writing and speaking. If you use a new term, then you'll really know it. In addition, studying new terms on flash cards or study sheets can be handy at exam time.

Reading Textbooks for Quantitative Courses

Reading Math Textbooks

Traditional textbooks in mathematics tend to have many symbols and fewer words than textbooks in humanities or social sciences. Each statement and every line in the solution of a problem is critically important and needs to be considered and digested slowly. Typically, the authors present the material through definitions, theorems, and sample problems. As you read, pay special attention to all the definitions. Learning all the terms in a new topic is the first step toward complete understanding.

Derivations of formulas and proofs of theorems are usually included to establish mathematical rigor. You must understand and be able to apply the formulas and theorems, but unless your course has an especially theoretical emphasis, you are less likely to be responsible for all the proofs. Thus, if you get lost in the proof of a theorem, go on to the next item in the section.

When you come to a sample problem, it's time to get busy. Pick up pencil and paper and work through the problem. Then look at the solution and think through the problem on your own. Of course, the exercises that follow each text section form the heart of any math book. A large portion of the time you devote to the course will be spent completing assigned textbook exercises.

To be successful in any math or science course, it is important that you keep up with all assignments. Don't allow yourself to fall behind. Do all your homework on time, whether or not your instructor collects it. After you complete the assignment, skim through the other exercises in the problem set. Just reading the unassigned problems will deepen your understanding of the topic and its scope. Finally, talk it through to yourself. As you do, focus on understanding the problem and its solution, not on memorization. Memorizing may help you recall how to work through one problem, but it does not help you understand the steps involved so that you can apply them to solving other problems.

Reading Science Textbooks

Your approach to your science textbooks will depend somewhat on whether you are studying a math-based

© Gary Connor/Getty Images

You're seriously shortchanging yourself if you don't complete your math and science homework problems on time.

science such as physics or a text-based science such as biology or zoology. In either case, you need to familiarize yourself with the overall format of the book. Review the table of contents and the glossary of terms. Check the material in the appendices. There you will find lists of physical constants, unit conversions, and various charts and tables. Many physics and chemistry books also include a brief review of the math you will need in science courses.

Read

Notice the organization of each chapter in the book and pay special attention to the graphs, charts, and boxes. At first the amount of technical detail may seem overwhelming, but realize that the authors have genuinely tried to present the material in an easy-to-follow format. Each chapter may begin with chapter objectives and conclude with a short summary, and you may wish to study both of these useful sections before and after reading the chapter. You will usually find answers to selected problems in the back of the book. Make sure that you understand how each problem was solved. Use the answer key and/or the student solutions manual in a responsible way to promote your mastery of each chapter.

As you begin an assigned section in a science text, skim the material quickly to get a general idea of the topic. Begin to absorb the new vocabulary and technical symbols. Then skim the end-of-chapter problems so you'll know what to look for as you do a second, and more detailed, reading of the chapter. State a specific goal—for example: "I'm going to learn about recent developments in plate tectonics," "I'm going to distinguish between mitosis and meiosis," "I'm going to learn about valence bond theory," or "Tonight I'll focus on the topics in this chapter that were stressed in class."

Should you underline and highlight in your science textbooks, or should you outline the material?

You may decide to underline or highlight in a subject such as anatomy, which involves a lot of memorization of terms. But be sure to use that highlighter with restraint; it should pull your eye only to important terms and facts. If highlighting is actually a form of procrastination for you (you are reading through the material but planning to learn it at a later date) or if you are highlighting nearly everything you read, your colorful pages of yellow, pink, or orange may be doing you more harm than good. When you reread the text before an exam, you won't be able to identify important concepts quickly if they're lost in a sea of color.

In most sciences, it is best to outline the text chapters. You can usually identify main topics, subtopics, and specific terms under each subtopic in your text by the size of the type. Headings printed in larger type will introduce major sections; smaller type is used for subtopics within these sections. To save time when you are outlining, don't write full sentences, but include clear explanations of new technical terms and symbols. Pay special attention to topics that were covered in the lecture class or in the lab. If you aren't sure whether your outlines contain too much or too little detail, compare them with those of a classmate or the members of your study group. In preparing for a test, it's a good idea to make condensed versions of your chapter outlines so that you can see how everything fits together.

Reading Textbooks for Social Science and Humanities Courses

Many of the suggestions that apply to science textbooks also apply to reading in the social sciences (sociology, psychology, anthropology, economics, political science, and history). Social science texts are filled with terms that are unique to the field of study. They also describe research and theory building and have references to many primary sources. Your social science texts may also describe differences in opinions or perspectives. Not all social scientists agree about any one issue, and you may be introduced to a number of ongoing academic debates. In fact, your reading can become more interesting if you seek out different opinions about a common issue. You may have to go beyond your textbook, and your campus library or the Internet will be good sources of various viewpoints about ongoing controversies.

Textbooks in the humanities (philosophy, religion, literature, music, and art) provide facts, examples, opinions, and original material such as stories and essays. You will often be asked to react to your reading by identifying central themes or characters.

Some professors believe that the way we structure courses and majors artificially divides human knowledge and experience. Those with this view may argue that subjects such as history, political science, and philosophy are closely linked and that studying each subject separately results in only partial understanding. These instructors will stress the connections between courses and encourage you to think in an interdisciplinary manner. You might be asked to consider how the book or story you're reading or the music you're studying reflects the political atmosphere or the prevailing culture of the period. Your art instructor may direct you to think about how a particular painting gives you a window on the painter's psychological makeup or religious beliefs.

© Stockbyte/SuperStock

Reading Primary Source Material

Whether or not your instructor requires you to read other material in addition to the textbook, your reading will be enriched if you track down some of the primary sources that are referenced in your text. These sources may be journal articles, research papers, dissertations (the major research papers that students write to earn a doctoral degree), laws, personal letters or diary entries, speeches, or original essays. These kinds of documents can be found in your library and increasingly on the Internet. Reading primary source material gives you a depth of detail and breadth of perspective that few textbooks provide.

Many primary sources were originally written to be read by other instructors or researchers. Therefore they often use language and refer to concepts that are familiar to other scholars but not necessarily to first-year college students. If you are reading a journal article that describes a theory or research study, one technique for easier understanding is to read from the end to the beginning. Read the article's conclusion and the "discussion" section and then go back to see how the experiment was done or the ideas were formulated. If you aren't concerned about the specific method used to collect the data, you can skip over the section on methodology.

In almost all scholarly journals, articles are introduced by an "abstract," a paragraph-length summary of the methods and major findings. Reading the abstract is a quick way to get the gist of a research article before you dive in. As you're reading research articles, always ask yourself, "So what?" Was the research important to what we know about the topic, or, in your opinion, was it unnecessary?

When the term ends, think before you sell your humanities or social science textbooks back to the bookstore. Literature, anthologies, books that explain timeless philosophical concepts, and overviews of historical periods may be valuable resources for you in the future—not just while you're in college, but even after you graduate. Even topics that seem irrelevant now may take on new meaning as you take more courses and gain life experience. And your college textbooks can be a foundation as you build your home library.

Where to Go for Help: Reading

On Campus

Learning assistance center: Most campuses have a learning center, and reading assistance is among its specialties. The best students, good students who want to be the best students, and students with academic difficulties all use learning centers. Services are offered by both full-time professionals and highly skilled student tutors.

Fellow college students: Often the best help we can get is the closest to us. Keep an eye out in your classes, residence hall, and campus groups of which you're a member for the best students—those who appear to be the most serious, purposeful, and directed. Hire a tutor. Join a study group. Students who do these things are much more likely to be successful.

Online

Middle Tennessee State University: http://www.mtsu.edu/~studskl/Txtbook.html. The "Study Skills Help" web page has a link to "Advice for Getting the Most from Reading Textbooks."

Niagara University's Office for Academic Support: http://www.niagara.edu/oas/learning_center/study_reading_strategies/reading.htm. View this website for "21 Tips for Better Textbook Reading."

TIPS

If English Is Not Your First Language

English is one of the most difficult languages to learn. Words are often spelled differently from the way they sound, and the language is full of idioms—phrases that are peculiar and cannot be understood from the individual meanings of the words. If you are a nonnative English speaker and are having trouble reading your texts, try these tips:

- Read slowly and read more than once to improve your comprehension.
- Have two good dictionaries at your fingertips—one in English and one that links English with your primary language—and look up every word that you don't know. One Web link you can use to help with translation is **http://www.foreignword.com/**.
- Practice thinking, writing, and speaking in English.
- Take advantage of your college's helping services. Your campus may have ESL (English as a Second Language) tutoring and workshops. Ask your adviser or your first-year seminar instructor to help you locate those services.

▶▶▶ BUILDING YOUR PORTFOLIO

The Big Picture

The more you read, the more things you will know.
The more you learn, the more places you'll go.

–Theodor Seuss Geisel, a.k.a. Dr. Seuss (1904–1991), American writer and cartoonist

In this step, you have been introduced to a reading strategy called **mapping** as a visual tool for getting the big picture of what you are preparing to read. Mapping a textbook chapter can help you quickly recognize how different concepts and terms fit together and make connections to what you already know about the subject. There are a number of ways mapping, including "wheel maps" and "branching maps." You might also use other types of maps, such as *matrices*, to compare and contrast ideas or show cause and effect; a *spider web* to connect themes; or *sketches* to illustrate images, relationships, or descriptions.

1. Create a new entry in your portfolio with the title "The Big Picture." Record your work for this assignment there.

2. Look through your course syllabi and identify a reading assignment that you need to complete in the next week.

   Which class are you preparing for?_____

3. Begin by previewing the first chapter of the reading assignment. Practice mapping the chapter by filling out the wheel map below or create your own version using the drawing toolbar in Microsoft Word. Attach it to your portfolio entry.

   Chapter title:_____

   a. Place the central idea of the chapter in the center of the wheel.

   b. Place supporting ideas on the "spokes" of the wheel.

   c. Place important details on the lines attached to the spokes.

Tip: A good place to start is with chapter headings and subheadings, then move on to terms in bold and graphics like charts, tables, and diagrams. Textbooks often have study questions at the end of the chapter; these can give you clues as to the most important concepts.

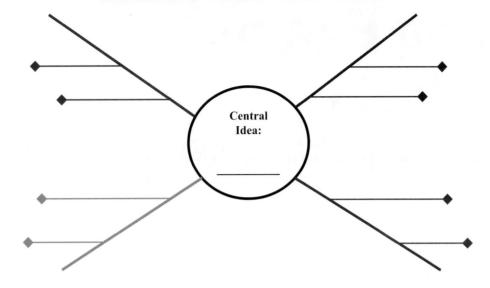

Optional: Create your own previewing map: map one chapter of your reading assignment, and include the document in your portfolio.

Reading a textbook efficiently and effectively requires that you develop reading strategies to make the most of your study time. Mapping can help you to organize and retain what you have read, making it a good reading and study tool. Writing, reciting, and organizing the main points, supporting ideas, and key details of the chapter will help you to recall the information on test day.

Taking Exams and Tests:

Putting All Your Essential Skills to the Test

You can prepare for test taking in many ways, using your preferred learning style to determine the approach that works best for you. In this step you'll find advice for preparing physically, emotionally, and academically.

You'll find that most college instructors emphasize high-level thinking skills such as analysis, synthesis, and evaluation. While they will expect you to remember material presented in lectures and the text, they will also frequently require you to provide the reasons, arguments, and assumptions on which a given position is based, and the evidence that confirms or discounts it. In exams as well as in other aspects of the course, instructors will want you to support your opinions and to show them how you think. ■

© F64/PhotoDisc Red/Getty Images

- how to prepare your mind and body for exams

- in what ways study groups and tutors can help you get ready for exams

- how you can prepare for the special demands of exams in math and science

- how using sound study techniques and tools throughout the academic term can increase your readiness for exams

- what steps you can take to improve your skill in remembering

- how to reduce test anxiety

- what strategies you can apply to do your best on tests

- how to answer different types of test questions

How Do You Measure Up?

Taking Exams and Tests

Check the following items that apply to you:

____ 1. I always begin studying for an exam at least a week in advance.

____ 2. I find that my class notes are very helpful when I'm preparing for an exam.

____ 3. I usually study for an exam with at least one other person.

____ 4. I know what to expect before I go into the exam.

____ 5. I study for tests by predicting possible questions and seeing whether I am prepared to answer them.

____ 6. I prepare for essay exams by predicting questions and developing outlines of the answers.

____ 7. I am careful to maintain good eating, sleeping, and exercise habits before exams.

____ 8. If I finish an exam early or on time, I recheck my answers.

____ 9. I read examination questions carefully so that I'm sure to give complete and precise answers.

____ 10. I seldom feel overly nervous when studying for or taking exams.

Review the items you did not check. Paying attention to all these aspects of your college experience can be very important to your success. After reading this step, come back to this list and choose an item or two that you did not check but are willing to work on.

Jeanne L. Higbee of the University of Minnesota, Twin Cities and Mary Ellen O'Leary of the University of South Carolina at Columbia contributed their valuable and considerable expertise to the writing of this section.

Planning Your Approach: The Long View

Prepare Ahead: Three Basic Steps

You actually began preparing for tests and examinations on the first day of the academic term. All of your lecture notes, assigned readings, and homework are part of that preparation. As the test day nears, you should know how much additional review time you will need, what material the test will cover, and what format the test will take. There are three basic steps you can take to prepare for tests:

1. Ask your instructor about the exam. Find out about the types of questions you'll have to answer, the time you will have to complete it, and the content to be covered. Ask how the exam will be graded and whether all questions will have the same point value.

2. Manage your time wisely. Create a schedule that will give you time to review for the exam over a period of time so that you don't end up waiting until the night before. Create a flexible schedule that allows for unexpected interruptions and distractions.

3. Sharpen your study habits. Determine how you can best review the material that is likely to be on the exam. If you like to collaborate with other students, have you worked in a study group or as study partners to share information? If you benefit from seeing the information you need to know visually, have you created maps, lists, diagrams, flash cards, tables, or other visual aids that will help you remember important information?

Prepare Physically

1. Maintain a regular sleep routine. Don't cut back on your sleep in order to cram in additional study hours. Remember that most tests will require you to be able to think clearly about the concepts that you have studied. Especially during final-exam weeks, you need to be well rested in order to remain alert and sharp for extended periods of time.

2. Follow a regular exercise program. Walking, running, swimming, and other aerobic activities are effective stress reducers. They provide positive—and needed—breaks from intense studying and may help you think more clearly.

3. Eat right. You really are what you eat (and drink). Avoid drinking too many caffeinated drinks and eating too much junk food. Be sure to eat breakfast before a morning exam. Ask the instructor if you can bring a bottle of water with you to the exam.

Prepare through Study with Others

1. Join a study group. Numerous research studies have shown that joining a study group is one of the most effective strategies for preparing for exams. Study groups can help you develop better study techniques. In addition, you can benefit from different views of your instructors' goals, objectives, and emphasis; have partners quiz you on facts and concepts; and gain the enthusiasm and friendship of others to help build and sustain your motivation.

Some professors allow class time for the formation of study groups. Otherwise, ask your instructor, adviser, or campus tutoring or learning center to help you identify interested students and decide on guidelines for the group. Study groups can meet throughout the term, or they can meet to review for midterms or final exams only. Team members should complete their assignments before the group meets, and should prepare study questions or points of discussion ahead of time. If your group decides to meet just before exams, allow enough time to share notes and ideas.

© Image 100/Alamy

Never pull an all-nighter before your exams. Be sure to catch your zs!

2. Get a tutor. Tutoring is not just for students who are failing. Often the best students seek tutorial assistance to ensure their As. In the typical large lecture classes for first-year students, you have a limited opportunity to ask instructors questions. Since many tutors are students who excelled in the same courses you are taking, they will be able to respond to your questions and give you advice on how to do well on exams. Most campus tutoring services are free. Consult with your academic adviser or counselor or the campus learning center.

Most academic support centers and learning centers have computer labs that can provide assistance for course work. Some offer walk-in assistance for help in using word processing, spreadsheet, or statistical computer programs. Often computer tutorials are available to help you refresh basic skills. Math and English grammar programs, as well as access to the Internet, may also be available.

Prepare Emotionally

1. Know the material. Study by testing yourself or by quizzing members of your study team so that you will be sure you really know the material. If you allow adequate time to review, you will enter the classroom on exam day confident that you are prepared.

2. Practice relaxing. If you experience an upset stomach, sweaty palms, a racing heart, or other unpleasant physical symptoms of test anxiety before an exam, see your counseling center about relaxation techniques. Practice them regularly. Some campus learning centers also provide workshops on reducing test anxiety.

3. Use positive self-talk. Instead of telling yourself, "I never do well on math tests" or "I'll never be able to learn all the information for my history essay exam," make positive statements such as "I have attended all the lectures, done my homework, and passed the quizzes. Now I'm ready to tackle and pass the test." This technique is called "cognitive restructuring." Make your self-messages encouraging rather than stress provoking.

Prepare for Math and Science Exams

More than in any other academic areas, your grades in math and science will be determined by your scores on major exams. To pass the course, you must perform well on timed tests. Here are suggestions for getting yourself fully prepared:

- Ask about test rules and procedures. Are calculators allowed? Are formula sheets permitted? If not, will any formulas be provided? Will you be required to give definitions? Derive formulas? State and/or prove theorems?

TRY IT!

Relaxing by Creating Your Own Peaceful Scene

Focus your thoughts on the most peaceful place you can imagine. It can be real or imaginary. It may be a place you remember fondly from your childhood, such as the park where your mother pushed you on a swing, or a special family vacation spot or a place where you always felt safe. Or it can be a place that you enjoy visiting now: the beach, the mountains, a cabin in the woods, a toasty fireplace on a cold day.

Now think about what you would hear, see, smell, taste, and feel if you were there right now. Think about not only how you would feel (optimally, relaxed!) but also what you would feel: the warmth of a fire, a gentle breeze, the sand between your toes. Now use all five senses to take yourself to your peaceful place. Just let yourself relax there for a while and get rid of any tension in your body. Practice this technique regularly, and you will be able to recreate your peaceful scene when you need to relax.

- Work as many problems as you can before the test. Practicing with sample problems is the best way to prepare for a problem-solving test.
- Practice understanding the precise meaning and requirements of problems. Failure to read problems carefully and to interpret and answer what is asked is the most common mistake for students taking science and math exams.
- Prepare in advance to avoid other common mistakes. Errors with parentheses (failing to use them when they are needed, failing to distribute a multiplier) and mistakes with negative signs are common in math-based courses. Pay attention in class to these details so that you don't fall into the typical traps when you are taking the exam.
- Study from your outline. In a subject such as anatomy, which requires memorizing technical terms and understanding the relationships among systems, focus your preparation on your study outline.
- Set high expectations for your performance. Think A all the way. Don't think, "What's the lowest grade I can make on the final to end up with a C in the course?"
- Take charge on test day. Arrive early and bring sharp pencils, erasers, a ruler, and fresh batteries for your calculator (if allowed). Skim the test. Gain confidence by first working the problems you know best, and then proceed to the ones you know second best. After that, divide your time according to the point value of the questions.

Using Other Study Strategies

If you consistently use good study techniques, you will process and learn most of what you need to know for exams as you go along. When exam time comes, you can focus on the most challenging concepts, practice recalling information, and familiarize yourself with essential details.

Review Sheets, Mind Maps, and Other Tools

To prepare for an exam covering large amounts of material, you need to condense the volume of notes and text pages into manageable study units. Review your materials with these questions in mind. Is this one of the key ideas in the chapter or unit? Will I see this on the test? You may prefer to highlight, underline, or annotate the most important ideas, or you may create outlines, lists, or visual maps containing the key ideas.

Use your notes to develop review sheets. Make lists of key terms and ideas that you need to remember. Also, do not underestimate the value of using a recall column from your lecture notes to test yourself or others on information presented in class. A recall column is a narrow space on the left side of your notebook paper that you can use to rewrite the ideas from the lecture that you most want to remember. A mind map, as shown here is essentially a review sheet with a visual element. Its word and visual patterns provide you with graphic clues to jog your memory. Because it is visual, the mind map approach helps many students recall information easily.

In addition to review sheets and mind maps, you may want to create flash cards. An advantage of flash cards is that you can keep them in an outside pocket of your backpack and pull them out to study anywhere. With flash cards you can make good use of precious minutes that otherwise might be wasted, such as time spent sitting on the bus or waiting for a friend.

Summaries of Course Material

Writing summaries of course topics can help you prepare to be tested, especially in essay and short-answer exams. By condensing the main ideas into a concise summary, you store information in your long-term memory so that you can retrieve it to answer an essay question. Here's how to create summaries:

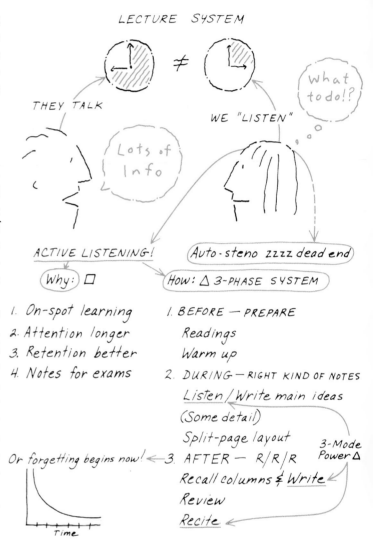

Mind maps can help you process information visually, for better recall.

1. Read the chapter, supplemental articles, notes, or other materials. Underline or mark main ideas as you go, make notations, or outline on a separate sheet of paper.

2. Predict a test question from your lecture notes or other resources. Look for instructor clues, such as repetition of an idea or fact.

3. Analyze and summarize. What is the purpose of the material? Does it compare, define a concept, or prove an idea? What are the main ideas? How would you explain the material to someone else?

4. Make connections between main points and key supporting details. Reread to identify each main point and supporting evidence. Create an outline to assist you in this process.

5. Select, condense, and order. Review material you have underlined, and write the ideas in your own words. Number what you have underlined or highlighted to put the material in a logical order.

6. Write your ideas precisely in a draft. In the first sentence, state the purpose of your summary. Follow this statement with each main point and its supporting ideas.

7. Review your draft. Read over your draft, adding missing transitions or insufficient information. Check the logic of your summary.

8. Test your memory. Put your draft away and try to recite the contents of the summary to yourself out loud, or explain it to a study partner who can provide feedback on the information you have omitted.

9. Schedule time to review your summaries, and test your memory shortly before the exam. You may want to review and test yourself with a partner, or you may prefer to review alone.

Exam Plans

Another useful way to study is to prepare an exam plan. Use the information about the test as you design a plan for preparing. Build that preparation into a schedule of review dates. Develop a "to-do" list of the major steps you need to take in order to be ready. During the week before the exam, set aside a schedule of one-hour blocks of time for review, and make notes on what you specifically plan to accomplish during each hour.

TRY IT!

Designing an Exam Plan

Use these guidelines to design an exam plan for one of your courses:

1. What type of exam will be used?
2. What material will be covered?
3. What type of questions will the exam contain?
4. How many questions will there be?
5. What approach will you use to study for the exam?
6. How many study sessions—and how much time—will you need?

Now list all material to be covered and create a study schedule for the week prior to the exam, allowing as many one-hour blocks as you believe you will need.

Where to Go for Help: Taking Exams and Tests

On Campus

Learning assistance support center: The best students, good students who want to be the best students, and students with academic difficulties use learning centers and tutoring services. These services are offered by both full-time professionals and student tutors.

Counseling services: College and university counseling centers offer a wide array of services, often including workshops and individual or group counseling for test anxiety.

Fellow college students: Keep an eye out for the best students, those who appear to be the most serious, purposeful, and directed. Seek the help of these classmates. Or hire a tutor or join a study group.

Online

Read the following two websites. Take notes. Write a summary of what you believe to be the important facts.

The Academic Center for Excellence, University of Illinois at Chicago: http://www.uic.edu/depts/ counselctr/ace/examprep.htm.

Learning Centre of the University of New South Wales in Sydney, Australia: http://www.lc.unsw.edu .au/onlib/exam.html.

Sharpening Your Memory

The benefits of having a good memory are obvious. In college, your memory will help you retain crucial information and score well on tests. After college, the ability to recall names, procedures, presentations, and appointments will save you energy, time, and a lot of potential embarrassment.

For many college courses, remembering concepts and ideas may be much more important than recalling details and facts. To embed main concepts and ideas in your mind, ask yourself these questions as you review your notes and books:

- What is the essence of the idea?
- Why does the idea make sense—what is the logic behind it?
- How does this idea connect to other ideas in the material?
- What might be the arguments against the idea?

Specific Aids to Memory

The human mind has discovered ingenious ways to remember information. Here are some tips that you may find useful as you're trying to sort out the causes of World War I, remember the steps in a chemistry problem, or absorb the complexities of a mathematical formula.

1. Pay attention to what you're hearing or reading. This suggestion is perhaps the most basic and the most important. If you're sitting in class thinking about everything except what the professor is saying, your memory doesn't have a chance. If you're reading and you find that your mind is wandering, you're wasting your study time. Force yourself to focus.

2. Don't rely on studying just once before an exam. Read and review class material many times, starting right after each class. The more often you review, the more likely the material will be "imprinted" on your brain. Avoid pre-exam all-nighters. Last-minute cramming, especially when it deprives you of sleep, is probably the worst thing you can do if you want to remember what you've read.

3. Analyze how you study and remember best. How are you most likely to remember what you hear and what you read? If you learn best by listening, tape your class lectures and replay them. If you need to be doing something in order to remember, stand up, sit on the edge of your chair, walk around, or gesture with your arms while you read and recite. Exerting energy while you study will keep you alert.

4. Say it over and over and aloud. Probably the most time-tested memory technique is reciting what you're trying to remember over and over out loud. Talking out loud is particularly important as an aid to memory, and it is more effective than reciting in your head. You'll need to use a study location where you're alone and won't bother others when you're "talking to yourself."

5. Work around what you are trying to remember. If your memory is stuck, try to recall related words or concepts. Brainstorm with yourself about everything you know related to that concept or person, and you'll most likely be able to remember the specific information you've temporarily forgotten.

6. Take notes on your notes. Some students find that they study and recall best by writing and rewriting. Rewriting the most important themes in your notes and taking additional notes on your reading material may help you remember what's most important.

7. Overlearn the material. After you know and think you understand the material you're studying, go over it again to make sure that you'll retain it for a long time.

STRATEGIES

Strategies For Remembering What May Be on the Test

- Pay close attention to what your instructors emphasize in class. Take good notes, and learn the material well before your exam. Unless they tell you otherwise, professors are quite likely to stress in-class material on exams.
- Review assigned readings before class and again after class, and note any material covered in both the reading assignments and class. You will likely see this material again—on your test.
- As you reread your notes, look for repeating ideas, themes, and facts. These are likely to appear on your test.
- Think and speak the key concepts and terminology of the course. The more your brain uses these ideas and words, the more you are likely to remember them.

Test yourself or ask someone else to test you. Recite what you're trying to remember aloud in your own words.

8. Consider joining a study group. Working with others to master and recall difficult material is a great way to remember more of the content over the long term. Group members can test each other and challenge each other's interpretation of the material. They can devise creative and even silly ways to remember.

9. Stay organized. If your desk, backpack, and computer are organized, you'll spend less time trying to remember a file name or where you put a particular document. And as you rewrite your notes, organize them in an order (either chronological or thematic) that makes sense to you so that you will more easily remember them.

10. Choose the right atmosphere for studying and remembering. Where do you concentrate most effectively—in your home or residence hall, in the library, in the campus center? Whatever the place, you need a quiet environment. Some people concentrate best in absolute quiet; others seem to benefit from having soft music playing in the background. Attempting to study in bed, in front of the TV, or while listening to loud music (or loud friends) is likely to be a waste of your study time.

11. Take advantage of Internet resources. If you're having trouble remembering what you have learned, try using a search engine such as Google to find additional details that may engage you in learning more about the subject. Many first-year courses cover such a large amount of material that you'll overlook the more interesting information—unless you seek it out and explore it for yourself. As your interest increases, so will your memory.

12. Try to reduce the stressors in your life. We don't know how much worry or stress causes you to forget, but most people agree that stress can be a distraction. Healthful, stress-reducing activities such as meditating, exercising, and getting enough sleep are especially important.

Stress can hinder your ability to remember, and yoga is a great activity for de-stressing.

Test

Facing Your Tests

Exam day has come, and you're mentally and emotionally prepared to be put to the test. Or are you? If you experience anxiety in association with taking exams and tests, you aren't alone.

Test anxiety is common and can manifest itself at many times and in many ways. Some students feel it on the first day of class. Other students begin showing symptoms of test anxiety when it is time to start studying for a test. Others do not get nervous until the night before the test or the morning of an exam day. And some students experience symptoms only while taking a test.

You can overcome test-taking anxiety by applying a mix of skills and knowledge. Here's how to keep this potentially powerful distracter at bay.

Applying Relaxation Strategies

In addition to studying hard, eating right, and getting plenty of sleep, simple strategies such as the following can help you overcome the physical and emotional impact of test anxiety.

- Any time that you begin to feel nervous or upset, take a long, deep breath and slowly exhale to restore your breathing to a normal rate.
- Before you go into the test room, especially prior to taking multi-hour final exams or sitting through several exams on the same day, stretch your muscles.
- When you sit down to take the test, relax your shoulders and back and keep your feet on the floor. Smooth out your facial muscles rather than wrinkling your forehead or frowning. Resist clenching your pencil or pen in your hand.
- Focus on the positive. If you tell yourself that you are not smart enough, that you did not study the right material, or that you are going to fail, turn those messages around.

Taking Any Test—Successfully

Use these general strategies as you take your seat and proceed with the test.

1. Write your name on the test. Always remember to write your name on the test and answer sheet (unless directed not to).

2. Analyze, ask, and stay calm. Read all the directions so that you understand what to do. Ask the instructor or exam monitor for clarification if you don't understand something. Be confident. Don't panic.

3. Use your time wisely. Quickly survey the entire test and decide how much time you will spend on each section. Be aware of the point values of different sections of the test.

4. Answer the easy questions first. Expect that you'll be puzzled by some questions. Make a note to come back to them later. If different sections consist of different types of questions (such as multiple-choice, short-answer, and essay), complete the types you are most comfortable with first. Be sure to leave enough time for any essays.

5. If you feel yourself starting to panic or go blank, stop whatever you are doing. Take a long, deep breath and slowly exhale. Remind yourself that you do know the material and can do well on this test. Then take another deep breath. If necessary, go to another section of the test and come back later to the item that triggered your anxiety.

6. If you finish early, don't leave. Stay and check your work for errors. Reread the directions one last time. If you are using an automatically gradable Scantron answer sheet, make sure that all your answers are filled in accurately and completely.

© BananaStock/SuperStock

Instructors sometimes allow open books or open notes during exams.

Test

Essay Questions

Many professors have a strong preference for essay exams for a simple reason: they promote critical thinking, whereas other types of exams tend to be exercises in memorization. To succeed on essay exams, follow these guidelines.

1. Budget your exam time. Quickly survey the entire exam, and note the questions that are the easiest for you, along with their point values. Take a moment to weigh their values, estimate the approximate time you should allot to each question, and write the time beside each item number. Be sure you understand whether you must answer all the questions or choose among questions. Remember that it can be a costly error to write profusely on easy questions of low value, taking up precious time you may need on more important questions. Wear a watch to monitor your time, remembering to include time at the end for a quick review.

2. Develop a very brief outline of your answer before you begin to write. First make sure that your outline responds to all parts of the question. Then use your first paragraph to introduce the main points, and subsequent paragraphs to describe each point in more depth. If you begin to lose your concentration, you will be glad to have the outline to help you regain your focus. If you find that you are running out of time and cannot complete an essay, at least provide an outline of key ideas. Instructors usually assign points based on your coverage of the main topics from the material. Thus, you will usually earn more points by responding to all parts of the question briefly than by addressing just one aspect of the question in detail.

3. Write concise, organized answers. Read each question carefully and pay attention to all its parts. Rather than hastily writing down everything you know on the topic, take the time to organize your thinking and to write a concise, well-structured answer. Instructors downgrade vague or rambling answers.

4. Know the key tasks in essay questions. The following key task words appear frequently on essay tests: *analyze, compare, contrast, criticize/critique, define, describe, discuss, evaluate, explain, interpret, justify, narrate, outline, prove, review, summarize,* and *trace.* Take time to learn them so that you can answer essay questions accurately and precisely.

Multiple-Choice Questions

Preparing for a multiple-choice test requires you to actively review all of the course material. Reciting from flash cards, summary sheets, mind maps, or the recall column in your lecture notes is a good way to review.

Take advantage of the many cues that multiple-choice questions contain. A careful reading of each item may reveal the correct answer. Be skeptical of choices that use absolute words such as *always, never,* and *only.* These choices are often (though not always) incorrect. Also, read carefully for terms such as *not, except,* and *but* that are introduced before the choices. Often the answer that is the most inclusive is correct.

Some students are easily confused by multiple-choice answers that sound alike. The best way to respond to a multiple-choice question is to read the first part of the question and then predict your own answer before reading the options. Choose the letter that corresponds with the answer that best matches your prediction.

Fill-in-the-Blank Questions

In many ways preparing for fill-in-the-blank questions is similar to getting ready for multiple-choice items. However, fill-in-the-blank questions are harder because you do not have a choice of possible answers right in front of you. Not all fill-in-the-blank questions are constructed the same way. Sometimes you'll see a series of blanks to give you a clue regarding the number of words in the answer, but sometimes one long blank is provided. If that is the case, you cannot assume that the answer is just one word.

True/False Questions

For the statement in a true/false question to be true, every detail of the statement must be true. As in multiple-choice tests, statements containing words such as *always, never,* and *only* are usually false, whereas less-definite terms such as *often* and *frequently* suggest the statement may be true. Read through the entire exam to see if information in one question will help you answer another. Do not second-guess what you know or doubt your answers just because a sequence of questions appears to be all true or all false.

Matching Questions

Matching questions are the hardest to answer by guessing. In one column you will find the terms; in the other, you see the descriptions of them. Before answering any question, review all of the terms and descriptions. Match those terms you are sure of first. As you do so, cross out both the term and its description, and then use the process of elimination to assist you in answering the remaining items.

WIRED WINDOW

EVEN IF YOU are typically enrolled in traditional face-to-face courses, you will undoubtedly take an increasing number of your exams online through course management systems (like eCollege and Blackboard). Some of the same tips for successful test taking also apply to online exams. Ensure that you will be in a quiet area free of distractions while you take the exam. Learn about constraints (e.g., time limit, due date) before the exam by asking your professor or logging in early to see if the constraints are posted online. If you haven't already done so, take a practice test so that you are familiar with the testing interface. If there is no time limit, take a break after you complete the exam and then go back and recheck your answers. If there is a time limit and the course management system does not show a timer, use a stopwatch or countdown timer to track your progress (a good rule of thumb is to have the countdown timer sound once with enough time left for you to review the entire exam and then again with 5 minutes left). Since you won't have a paper exam, you'll be unable to take notes on the exam itself. Be prepared to have a notepad with you to jot down notes. You also won't be able to easily move back and forth between the pages of the exam to review your answers or skip questions for later. Therefore, when reviewing your answers or going back to previous questions, make sure that you have saved every page of the exam. If you save your exam and have not yet submitted it for grading, you can use your browser's back button to review questions and answers on previous pages.

▶▶▶ BUILDING YOUR PORTFOLIO

A High Price to Pay

I desire so to conduct the affairs of this administration that if at the end,
when I come to lay down the reins of power, I have lost every other friend on earth,
I shall at least have one friend left, and that friend shall be down inside me.

—Abraham Lincoln (1809–1865), sixteenth President of the United States

Do you know the meaning of the words "academic integrity"? Academic integrity is a supreme value on college and university campuses. Faculty, staff, and students are held to a strict code of academic integrity, and the consequences of breaking that code can be severe and life-changing. Create a new entry in your portfolio with the title "A High Price to Pay." Record your work for this assignment there.

1. Imagine that you have been hired by your college or university to conduct a month-long academic integrity awareness campaign so that students will learn about and take your campus's guidelines for academic integrity seriously. To prepare for your new job,

   a. Visit your institution's website and use the search feature to find the Academic Integrity Code/Policy. Take time to read through the code, violations, and sanctions. Enter the website link here so it will be easy to find later:

   _____

   b. Visit the judicial affairs office on your campus to learn more about the way your institution deals with violations of academic integrity policies.

   c. Research other online resources, such as the Center for Academic Integrity, hosted by Clemson University (**www.academicintegrity.org**), and read about its Fundamental Values Project.

   d. Check out other colleges' and universities' academic integrity codes and/or honor codes. How do they compare to your institution's code or policy?

2. Outline your month-long awareness campaign and include it in your portfolio.

   Here are a few ideas to get you started:

   Plan a new theme every week; don't forget Internet-related violations.

   Develop eye-catching posters to display around campus. For samples, check out the posters designed by students at Elizabethtown College in Pennsylvania (**www.rubberpaw.com/integrity**).

   Think about guest speakers, debates, skits, or other presentations.

   Come up with catchy slogans or phrases.

   Send students a postcard highlighting your institution's policies or honor code.

   Consider the most effective ways to communicate your message to different groups on campus.

You might want to share your campaign ideas with other students in your class and even select the best ideas for presentation to your campus student affairs office or judicial board.

Relationships,
Diversity, and Values:

Understanding and Respecting Yourself and Others

© Stockbyte/Picture Quest

As a college student, are classes and studies the first things on your mind? Your instructors may think so. Your family may hope so. But student journals suggest that what often takes center stage are relationships—with dates, lovers, or lifelong partners; with friends and enemies; with parents and family; with roommates, classmates, and co-workers; and with new people and new groups.

Some of the people with whom you form relationships will come from different cultural and social backgrounds, and you may be exposed to more diversity than you experienced before college. They may hold values that are different from your own. What's more, your values and those of your friends may change during college. Learning to get along with a wide range of people from diverse backgrounds and with different values is an important lesson for college, for any job you may hold in the future, and for other aspects of your life. ■

In this step you will learn:

- why and how your various personal relationships are important to your success in college

- how to determine whether a serious relationship is right for you

- how to recognize and deal with intimate-partner violence in a relationship

- in what ways relationships with parents or family members change when you are attending college

- what diversity and multicultural education mean in a college setting

- what are the appropriate, and the most personally beneficial, ways to approach campus diversity

- what we mean by "values"

- how to distinguish among moral, aesthetic, and performance values

- how to distinguish between means values and ends values

How Do You Measure Up?

Relationships, Diversity, and Values

Check the following items that apply to you:

____ 1. I am aware of the pros and cons of getting romantically involved while I'm in college.

____ 2. I understand the difficulties of maintaining a long-distance relationship.

____ 3. I know what to do and what resources are available if I ever find myself in a relationship that is emotionally, verbally, or physically abusive.

____ 4. I have established ground rules for living together with my roommate.

____ 5. I understand how to maintain good communication with my family while I'm in college.

____ 6. I know what it takes to be a good friend.

____ 7. I know how electronic relationships can be both valuable and dangerous.

____ 8. I seek opportunities to learn about cultures that are different from my own.

____ 9. I have good friends who are from other cultures, races, and age groups or who may have a different sexual orientation than my own.

____ 10. When some aspect of a friend's behavior clashes with my personal values, I know what to do and what not to do.

Review the items you did not check. Paying attention to all these aspects of your college experience can be very important to your success. After reading this step, come back to this list and choose an item or two that you did not check but are willing to work on.

John M. Whiteley and James B. Craig, University of California, Irvine, and Tom Carskadon of Mississippi State University contributed their valuable and considerable expertise to the writing of this section.

101

Developing Healthy Romantic Relationships

Not only does college present an opportunity to make new friends, it is also a place where romantic relationships can flourish. Although some college students are married or in a long-term committed relationship, others may have their first serious romance with someone they meet on campus. Whether you are straight, gay, lesbian, bisexual, or transgendered, you may find it much easier to meet romantic partners during college than ever before.

Through these relationships, you'll learn a great deal about yourself and those with whom you become involved. You may also get insight on what it would be like to live with or marry your partner before you take that life-changing step.

You may have a relationship you feel is really special. Should you make it exclusive? Don't do so just because being with each other exclusively has become a habit. Ask yourself why you want this relationship to be exclusive. For security? To prevent jealousy? To build depth and trust? As a prelude to a permanent commitment? Before you decide to see only each other, make sure this choice is best for each of you. You may find that you treat each other better and appreciate each other more when you feel free to explore other relationships.

If you are seriously thinking about marriage or a long-term commitment, consider this: Studies show that the younger you are, the lower your odds of a successful marriage. Also, living together before getting married does not decrease your risk of later divorce.

Above all, beware of what might be called the fundamental marriage error: marrying before both you and your partner are certain about who you are and what you want to do in life. Many people change their outlook and life goals drastically as time passes. If you want to marry, the person to marry is someone you can call your best friend—the one who knows you inside and out, the one you don't have to play games with, the one who prizes your company, the one who over a period of years has come to know, love, and respect who you are and what you want to be.

Long-Distance Relationships

Relationships change significantly when they turn into long-distance romances. Many students arrive at college while still romantically involved with someone back home or at another college.

College is an exciting setting with many social opportunities. If you restrict yourself to a single, absent partner, you may miss out on a lot and consequently grow resentful or begin cheating. If you are in a long-distance relationship, your best option may be to keep seeing your significant other as long as you want to, but with the freedom to pursue other relationships. If

College provides an environment where relationships of all kinds flourish.

© Creatas/Photolibrary USA

Looking for Love

Read the personal ads in your campus or local newspaper. Write down the questions, issues, and themes that people seem to be writing about most. What does this information tell you about what people value most in relationships?

the best person for you turns out to be the person from whom you are separated, you will know as time goes on, and you can reevaluate the situation. Meanwhile, keep your options open.

Breaking Up

If it is time to end a relationship, do it cleanly and calmly. Don't be impulsive or angry. Explain your feelings and talk them out. If you get an immature or a nasty reaction, take the high road; don't join someone else in the mud. If you decide to reunite after a trial separation, allow enough time to pass for you to evaluate the situation with some perspective. If the relationship fails a second time, you need to move on.

If your partner breaks up with you, you may feel sad, angry, or even depressed. Remember that you're not alone. Almost everyone has been rejected or "dumped" at one time or another. Let some time pass, be open to moral support from your friends and your family, and, if necessary, pay a visit to your college counselor or a chaplain. These skilled professionals have assisted many students through similar experiences, and they can be there for you as well. Bookstores and your library will have good books on surviving a breakup. You may wish to remain friends with your former partner, especially if you have shared and invested a lot in your relationship. It will be difficult to be friends, however, until both of you have healed from the hurt and neither of you wants the old relationship back.

Intimate-Partner Violence

Emotional or verbal abuse or violent acts between two people who care deeply for each other are called intimate-partner violence. About one-third of all college-age students will experience a violent intimate relationship, and women aged sixteen to twenty-four experience the highest rates of such abuse.

It's important to recognize the warning signs and know what to do if you find yourself in an abusive relationship:

- You're frightened by your partner's temper and afraid to disagree.
- You apologize to others for your partner's abusive behavior.
- You avoid family and friends because of your partner's jealousy.
- You're afraid to say "no" to sex even if you don't want it.
- You're forced to justify everything you do, everywhere you go, and everyone you see.
- You're the object of ongoing verbal insults.
- You've been hit, kicked, shoved, or had things thrown at you.

If you have experienced any of this, tell your abuser the violence must stop. If you are in immediate danger, call 911 or the campus police. But also contact campus resources such as women's student services, call a community domestic violence center or rape crisis center, or find a counselor or support group on campus or in the community. You even can obtain a restraining order through your local magistrate or county court. If the abuser is a student at your school, schedule an appointment with your campus judicial officer to explore campus disciplinary action.

Relate

Maintaining Other Important Relationships

Parents

Whether you live on campus or at home, becoming a college student right after you leave high school will change your relationship with your parents. Home will never be quite the same, and you will not be who you were before. You may find that your parents try to make decisions on your behalf, such as what major you should choose, where and how much you should work, and what you should do on weekends. You also may find that it's hard for you to make any decisions without talking to your parents first. While communication with your parents is important, your college or university advisers or counselors can help you draw the line between what decisions should be yours alone and what decisions your parents should help you make.

Many college students are living in blended families, so that more than one set of parents is involved in their college experience. If your father or mother has remarried or has a new partner, you may have to negotiate with both family units.

A first step in ensuring a positive relationship with your parents is to be aware of their concerns and feelings. These are the most common:

- Parents fear you'll make bad decisions such as drinking too much or engaging in behaviors they don't approve of. You may take risks that your elders would not take or risks that no one should take.
- Parents think their daughter is still a young innocent. The old double standard (differing expectations for men than women, particularly regarding sex) is alive and well.
- Parents know you're older but may continue to see you as a child. Somehow, the parental clock always lags behind reality.
- Parents fear that you might change in some negative way and lose the values of your family and culture.
- Parents worry that you may never live at home again, and for some college students, this is exactly what happens.

Parents often have genuine concerns. To help them feel comfortable with your life in college, try setting aside regular times to update them on how college and your life in general are going. Ask for and consider their advice—even if you end up not taking it.

Spouses, Partners, and Families

If you live with a spouse, partner, or children of your own, your college transition will not only affect you, but them as well. They may have concerns and fears about whether and how you will change, and your responsibilities to them will certainly add to your time management challenges. But families can also be a special source of support as you pursue your academic goals. Help them feel a part of the college experience by including them in campus activities designed for family members. Spend time sharing your hopes and dreams, and let them know how your college success will make a positive difference for everyone in the family

Roommates

If you live on campus, adjusting to a roommate is a significant transition experience. You may make a friend for life—or an acquaintance you wish you'd never known. A roommate doesn't have to be a best friend, just someone with whom you can comfortably share your living space. Your best friend may not make the best roommate.

© Steve/Mary Skjold/Photolibrary USA

Being a college student changes the relationship with parents and requires adjustments on both sides.

Relate

With roommates, it's important to establish your mutual rights and responsibilities. If you have problems, talk them out promptly. Speak directly—politely but plainly. If your problems persist, or if you don't know how to address them, seek professional counseling, which usually is available free of charge at your campus's counseling center. Normally, you can tolerate (and learn from) a less than ideal situation. But if things get really bad and do not improve, insist on a change.

Friends

One of the best parts of going to college is meeting new people. Studies of college students have found that they learn more from other students than they learn from professors. Although not everyone you hang out with will be a close friend, you will likely form some special relationships that may even last a lifetime.

Choose your friends carefully. You are who you associate with—or you soon will be. If you want a friend, be a friend. Here's how:

- Be an attentive listener.
- Give your opinion when asked.
- Keep your comments polite and positive.
- Never violate a confidence.
- Offer an encouraging word and a helping hand when you can.

Your friends usually have attitudes, goals, and experiences similar to your own. But in your personal life, just as in class, you have the most to learn from people who are different from you. You'll find it an enriching experience to diversify—to make friends with students who come from another state or country, are from a different racial or ethnic group, or are of a different sexual orientation or age.

Electronic Relationships

Through email, interest groups, and dating sites, it is possible to form relationships with people you have never met. Today, many students are using online directories such as Facebook to meet and interact with other students. Forming virtual social relationships can be fun as well as educational.

The downside? Electronic relationships may be brief and less predictable than "real world" ones. People may not be what they seem. Meeting them in real life may be delightful—or disastrous. Some people assume false electronic identities. You could be corresponding with someone who might not have the best intentions toward you. Be very cautious about letting strangers know your name, address, telephone number, and other personal information.

If you find yourself spending hours every day interacting with people on the computer, you're probably overdoing it. You don't want to let your electronic associations substitute for other relationships in your life. But as a way to meet interesting people and stay in touch with distant contacts and friends, electronic relationships can be uniquely valuable.

Where to Go for Help: Relationships

On Campus

Counseling center: Professional college counselors help students think and talk about their relationships and support and advise them regarding the most appropriate courses of action. This kind of counseling is strictly confidential (unless you are a threat to the safety of yourself or others) and usually is provided at no charge. But, unless your situation is an emergency, be prepared to wait for your first appointment, as these centers have very heavy caseloads due to an increase in student stressors.

Chaplains: An often underrecognized resource in terms of getting help on relationship matters is a campus chaplain. Almost all colleges, both public and private, have religiously affiliated ministerial chaplains, who usually have specialized training in pastoral counseling.

Student organizations: The variety of student groups designed to bring together students to help them with their relationships is virtually unlimited. You may find everything from Greek letter social fraternities and sororities to associations for single parents with children or for gay/lesbian/bisexual/transgendered students.

Your academic adviser: Even though your adviser may not have the exact expertise you seek, he can refer you to the proper person or office.

Online

The University of Chicago's "Student Counseling Virtual Pamphlet Collection": http://counseling .uchicago.edu/resources/virtualpamphlets/ relationships.shtml. This website takes you to dozens of websites about problems in relationships. You can browse the many links for information of interest.

Healthy Romantic Relationships during College: http://www.utexas.edu/student/cmhc/booklets/ romrelations/romrelations.html. The University of Texas Counseling Center offers an online brochure that explores the ups and downs of romantic relationships.

Understanding Diversity

Diversity is the variety of social, ethnic, and cultural identities among people coexisting in a defined setting. As your higher education experience unfolds, you'll find yourself immersed in this mixture of identities. Going to college brings together people with differing backgrounds and life experiences but with common goals and aspirations. Each person brings to campus a unique life story, upbringing, value system, view of the world, and set of judgments. You can tap these differences to enhance your experiences in the classes you take, the organizations you join, and the relationships you cultivate.

As you encounter new situations and new people, avoid making assumptions about them based on stereotypes. Stereotyping is not only unfair to others but it also denies you the opportunity to get to know others as unique individuals.

Race, Ethnicity, and Culture

Let's start with a few definitions. "Race" (for example, Caucasian, Asian) generally refers to biological characteristics shared by groups of people and includes hair texture and color, skin tone, and facial features. "Ethnicity" refers to a quality assigned to a specific group of people who are historically connected by a common national origin or language. For example, Latinos are a large ethnic group whose members come from over thirty countries, from North America to the Caribbean, all of whom share the Spanish language. These countries also share many traditions and beliefs, though with some variations. "Ethnic group" can refer to people of different races who can be distinguished by their language and national origin, or to people of the same race who can be distinguished in these ways. "Culture" encompasses those aspects of a group of people that are passed on and/or learned. Traditions, foods, language, clothing styles, artistic expression, and beliefs are all a part of culture.

Given the existence of considerable diversity within racial, ethnic, and cultural groups, making assumptions and generalizations about group identity based on traits can do more harm than good. Try to become aware of the variations of race, ethnicity, and culture on and off campus. No one would expect you to be an expert, now or in the future. In fact, with so much variation within groups, thinking that you have it all figured out would be fooling yourself. The best

TRY IT!

Evaluating Diversity on Your Campus

What efforts does your college or university take to ensure that students feel welcome? Enrollment statistics are typically available from the campus's office of institutional research and are usually accessible online. What do the data say about which groups are well represented at your campus? Which groups are not? Make lists for both. What steps does the college take to increase diversity?

approach is to avoid making quick judgments about people and to avoid assigning group labels.

Evidence indicates that social interaction in a diverse setting can significantly improve your education. What's more, both for students preparing to enter the labor force in the near future and for returning students who are or have been employed, interacting respectfully with people from diverse racial, ethnic, cultural, and economic backgrounds can significantly enhance success on the job.

Differences in Sexual Orientation

In college you will likely meet both students and professors who are homosexual or bisexual. Because most colleges are inclusive of gay, lesbian, or bisexual people, many individuals who were "in the closet" in high school will come out in the collegiate environment. Sexual orientation is a personal and often emotionally charged characteristic, but whatever your sexual orientation, it is important that you respect all individuals with whom you come in contact.

Returning Students

Adult students of age twenty-five and older are enrolling in college courses in record numbers. Parents may decide to return to college after raising children, to learn skills for a new career, or to update skills they have. Others may decide it's time to broaden their horizons or prepare for a better job with a higher starting salary. Many returning students work full time and attend school part time. Their persistence is remarkable, given the potential stressors of family and work. But one study discovered that older women in college experienced less stress than younger students, partly because they had grown accustomed to wearing two or more hats while raising children, working, and living their own lives. Colleges

Relate

have accommodated the needs of returning students by offering distance education courses, night courses, weekend courses, and entire degree programs online.

Students with Disabilities

Students with learning disabilities have trouble learning certain academic skills, such as listening, thinking, speaking, writing, spelling, or doing math calculations. The number of such students continues to grow. Although they lack abilities in some areas, students with learning disabilities are usually of normal or above-average intelligence and are motivated to learn coping strategies that aid them in dealing with different types of academic situations. Most learning disabilities are not readily apparent. If a friend confides that he is having difficulty with one or more skills that seem basic to you, you might urge him to consult with your campus's academic skills center.

Unlike learning disabilities, most physical disabilities are apparent. When you see a student or faculty member with a physical disability, the most respectful thing to do is to treat the person as you would anyone else. If a student in one of your classes has a physical impairment, you probably should not go out of your way to offer help unless the person asks for it; overeagerness to help may be seen as an expression of pity. Most campuses have a special office to serve students with physical disabilities and learning disabilities.

Discrimination, Prejudice, and Insensitivity on Campuses

College and university campuses are not immune to acts of discrimination and prejudice. The college campus is a unique setting where diverse groups of people interact and share physical as well as psychological space. Unfortunately,

© Bonnie Kamin/PhotoEdit

Being a parent while going to college is a major challenge.

TRY IT! **Looking at the Curriculum**

At this point, you may have identified some majors that interest you. Using your campus's course catalog, identify and list courses in those majors that focus on the topics of multiculturalism and diversity. Why do you think academic departments have included these topics in the curriculum? How would studying diversity and multiculturalism help you prepare for the field of your choice?

there are those who do not value diversity, but instead choose to respond negatively to groups that differ from their own. Acts of discrimination and prejudice have been documented on campuses across the country.

Colleges and universities work continually to ensure a welcoming and inclusive campus environment for all students, current and prospective. Specialized campus resources focus on providing support to, and acknowledgment of, the diverse student population. Campus administrations have established policies against all forms of discriminatory behavior, racism, and insensitivity, and many campuses have zero-tolerance policies that prohibit verbal and nonverbal harassment, intimidation, and violence.

Find out what resources are available on your campus to protect you and others from discriminatory and racist behavior. Also learn what steps your college or university takes to promote the understanding of diversity and multiculturalism—the active process of acknowledging and respecting the various social groups, cultures, religions, races, ethnicities, attitudes, and opinions. If you are ever the victim of a racist, insensitive, or discriminatory act while in college, report it to the proper campus authorities.

A Final Look at Diversity

Diversity enriches everyone. Allowing yourself to become more culturally aware and open to differing views will help you become truly educated. Understanding the value of working with others and the importance of open-mindedness will enhance your educational and career goals and provide gratifying experiences both on and off campus. Making the decision to pursue a genuinely multicultural education is just that, a decision—one that will require you to be active and sometimes to step out of your comfort zone. There are many ways for you to become more culturally aware, with a variety of opportunities on your campus. From concerts to films, guest speakers to information tables, you may not have to go far to gain insight into diversity.

Relate

Exploring Your Values and the Values of Others

As well as an opportunity for exposing you to the values of others, college is a time for exploring your own values. The word "values" means different things to different people. For some, the word refers to the specific views a person holds about a controversial moral issue, such as capital punishment. For others, it refers to whatever is most important to a person, such as a good job, a high-performance car, or the welfare of one's family. For still others, it refers to abstractions such as truth, justice, and success. Perhaps we can best define a value as an important attitude or belief that commits us to take action. We may not necessarily act in response to others' feelings, but when we truly hold a value, we act on it.

We can also define values as beliefs that we accept by choice, with a sense of responsibility and ownership. Much of what we think is simply what others have taught us. Many things we have learned from our parents and others close to us will count as our values, but only after we fully embrace them ourselves. You must personally accept or reject something before it can become a value for you.

The idea of affirming or prizing is an essential part of values. When we affirm and prize our values, we proudly declare them to be true, we readily accept the choices to which they lead, and we want others to know it. We also find ourselves ready to sacrifice for our values and to establish our priorities around them. Our values govern our loyalties and commitments.

Types of Values

There are a number of useful ways to think about values in practice. One approach is to distinguish among moral values, aesthetic values, and performance values. Another is to consider means values versus ends values.

Moral values Our moral values are those personal values that we generally do not attempt to force on others but that are of immense importance to ourselves as individuals. An example of a moral value is believing that it is wrong to lie because lying shows disrespect for other people.

We use moral values to justify our own behavior toward others, as well as to privately judge others. The college years represent a significant opportunity to focus on the choice of moral values to live by—often, for the first time, away from the influences of parents, siblings, and previous peer groups.

Aesthetic values The standards by which we judge beauty are aesthetic values. Beauty, as used here, refers to a broad set of judgments about nature, art, music, literature, personal appearance, and so on. For example, people make different value judgments about what kind of music is good, what is of value artistically, and what types of books are worth reading. Within society there are vast differences of opinion about how to define proper aesthetic values and how to judge beauty— or even what beauty is.

Performance values There is comparatively less disagreement about non-moral performance values— how well a person performs to some standard—at least on most campuses and within other institutional cultures. The definition of performance may vary from person to person or context to context, but some representative performance values include accuracy,

© PhotoDisc/Getty Images

Having a set of values that genuinely makes sense to you is important for navigating life.

Relate

speed, accomplishment, reward, and discipline. Performance values influence college students through the expectations held by other important people in their lives. No example is closer to home for college students than the expectations of parents and professors for a high level of academic performance. In addition, some significant others tend to make negative evaluations when a partner does not measure up to their own performance standards.

Ends values and means values Alternatively, we may classify values as "ends values" or "means values." Ends values, or intrinsic values, refer to the ultimate goals worth striving for. According to the late psychologist Milton Rokeach, ends values include world peace, a comfortable life, freedom, wisdom, and true friendship. Means values, or instrumental values, are values one uses to attain other values. Rokeach identified eighteen means values, ranging from being responsible, obedient, loving, and imaginative to being ambitious, independent, and honest.[1]

But values do not always separate clearly into means and ends categories. The fundamental American value of equality of opportunity, for example, is frequently offered as an intrinsic value of our society and one of the values that distinguishes the United States from totalitarian countries. But equality of opportunity can also be instrumental to the achievement of other intrinsic values, such as the enhancement of human dignity, the realization of human potential, and the liberation of the human spirit, and this quality puts it in the category of a means value.

Challenges to Personal Values in College

Most students find that college life challenges their existing personal and moral values. New students are often startled at the diversity of personal moralities found on campus. For instance, you may have been taught that it is wrong to drink alcohol, yet you may find that friends whom you respect and care about see nothing wrong with drinking. At the same time, if you come from a liberal background, you may be astonished to discover yourself forming a friendship with classmates who have very conservative personal values.

When you don't approve of some aspects of a friend's way of life, do you try to change her behavior, pass judgment on her, or withdraw from the relationship? If you find that question hard to answer, it may be because the friend demonstrates countless good qualities and values that make the troublesome conduct seem less significant. In the process, your own values may begin to change under the influence of a new kind of relativism: "I don't choose to do that, but I'm not going to make any judgments against those who do."

In cases when a friendship is affected by differing values, tolerance is generally a good goal. Tolerance for others is a central value in our society and one that often grows during college. Even so, it is easy to think of cases in which tolerance gradually becomes an indulgence of another's destructive tendencies. It is one thing to accept a friend's responsible use of alcohol at a party, and quite another to fail to challenge a drunk who plans to drive you home. Sexual intimacy in an enduring relationship may be one thing; a never-ending series of one-night stands is quite another. Remember, the failure to challenge destructive conduct is no sign of friendship.

Your challenge is to balance your personal welfare, your tolerance for others' behavior, and your freedom of choice. It can be very enriching and rewarding to talk about values with those whose values seem to be in conflict with your own. You can learn a great deal from discussing what you value, and why, with others. Yet some people avoid confronting different value systems, even though, realistically speaking, the values of our society change over time and many deeply held societal values are in serious conflict. Adopting a set of values that truly makes sense to you can help you to move ahead with your life and to consciously analyze and reflect on what is taking place in society.

Relate

---

[1]M. Rokeach, *Understanding Human Values: Individual and Societal* (New York: The Free Press, 1979).

WIRED WINDOW

IN A RECENT SURVEY, between 3 and 10 percent of college students lied on their social networking website profiles about their age, gender, what they do for a living, or their interests. The popular media frequently report on people who use social networking websites to prey on others. A recent investigation by a popular news magazine found that almost 750 registered sex offenders had MySpace profiles. Imagine how many offenders are on MySpace who don't list their real names. Even though the percentage of people who use MySpace to prey on others is small relative to the number of total users, it is important to consider ways of protecting yourself. Use common-sense precautions (like not giving out your location or contact information) and adjust your privacy settings accordingly. As the aforementioned survey found, the level of deceit on social networking sites varies based on the significance of the lie the person is telling. The chances that people will lie about a criminal background are greater than the chances they will lie about their age or gender. Even if you are careful to avoid offenders online, you can be hurt emotionally by someone who is deceitful. You might already know people who found that some of their MySpace friends weren't who they thought they were. Try your own MySpace investigation. Find a MySpace profile of someone you think is not who they portray themselves to be. What are your reasons for selecting this profile? Why do you think this person is representing himself or herself in this way?

▶▶▶ BUILDING YOUR PORTFOLIO

A Day in the Life

*To exist is to change, to change is to mature, to mature
is to go on creating oneself endlessly.*

—Henri Bergson (1859–1941), French philosopher

Managing family relationships while in college can sometimes be a real challenge! Whether you attend college in your hometown or across the country, relationships with those who are close to you will change. Sometimes parents or other family members have a hard time letting go, and sometimes it is difficult for new college students to start making independent decisions.

1. Create a new entry in your portfolio with the title "A Day in the Life." Record your work for this assignment there.

2. Describe some of the ways your life has changed since coming to college (e.g., more independence, personal responsibility, less free time). How have you handled these changes? What has been the most difficult aspect of your new college life so far?

3. Have you considered how your family's day-to-day lives might also have changed since you began college? Conduct an in-person or phone interview with one (or more) of your family members about how life has changed for them.

   Tip: Set up a mutually convenient time to talk and choose a quiet place, free of distractions.

Here are a few questions to get you started:

   a. What do you feel has changed in your life since I began college?

   b. Is the family routine any different now?

   c. Do you worry about me? If so, what is your biggest concern about my college experience?

   d. Do you feel like we communicate enough (by phone, email, etc.)?

If possible, insert photos of the people you interview here.

4. Reflect on what you learned from the interviews. How can you be sensitive to your family's needs/concerns while recognizing your own changing needs?

Staying Healthy:

Managing Stress and Achieving Wellness

© Big Cheese Photo/SuperStock

Physical fitness is one of many keys to wellness.

College provides countless opportunities to exercise your mind and expand your horizons. Unfortunately, while college students exercise their minds, many neglect to exercise their bodies. Sometimes they also experiment with a variety of risky behaviors. While most students find healthy ways to cope with the transition to college, some become so stressed that their anxiety overwhelms them. Others ignore the consequences of their sexual decisions and end up getting a sexually transmitted infection or facing an unplanned pregnancy. Some students drink too much, smoke, or abuse drugs. If you fail to take care of your mind and body while you're in college, you can seriously compromise your health, well-being, academic performance, and future.

This step explores the topic of "wellness," which is a broad term for a healthy mind, body, and spirit. Wellness involves making healthy choices and achieving a balance among all aspects of your life. Attaining wellness means reducing stress, eating a healthy diet, keeping fit, maintaining sexual health, and taking a sensible approach to alcohol, tobacco, and other drugs. ∎

In this step you will learn:

- why managing stress is important

- how you can manage stress by paying attention to your diet, exercise, sleep, and relaxation needs

- what options you have for contraception and safer sex

- how to avoid getting a sexually transmitted infection (STI)

- what symptoms indicate that you or someone you know might have an STI

- what we know about alcohol use and smoking among college students

- what consequences result from the abuse of prescription drugs and the use of illegal drugs

How Do You Measure Up?

Staying Healthy

Check the following items that apply to you:

____ 1. When I feel overwhelmed, I deal with my stress in healthy ways, like taking a walk or exercising.

____ 2. Although I am busy, taking care of my physical health is always a priority.

____ 3. I am conscientious about getting enough sleep, even on nights before exams.

____ 4. I exercise regularly and manage my weight to stay fit.

____ 5. I have adequate information about sex and contraception.

____ 6. I know how to avoid contracting a sexually transmitted infection.

____ 7. I don't have to drink alcohol in order to have fun.

____ 8. I know the difference between responsible and irresponsible alcohol use.

____ 9. I don't use tobacco products, even in moderation.

____ 10. I understand the consequences of abusing legal and illegal drugs.

Review the items you did not check. Paying attention to all these aspects of your college experience can be very important to your success. After reading this step, come back to this list and choose an item or two that you did not check but are willing to work on.

Michelle Murphy Burcin of the University of South Carolina at Columbia contributed her valuable and considerable expertise to the writing of this section.

Recognizing the Effects of Stress

When you are experiencing stress, your body undergoes rapid physiological, behavioral, and emotional changes. Your rate of breathing may become more rapid and shallow. Your heart rate speeds up, and the muscles in your shoulders, forehead, the back of your neck, and perhaps across your chest tighten. Your hands may become cold and/or sweaty. You may experience disturbances in your gastrointestinal system, such as "butterflies" in your stomach, diarrhea, or constipation. Your mouth and lips may feel dry and hot, and you may notice that your hands and knees begin to shake or tremble. Your voice may quiver or even go up to a higher pitch.

A number of psychological changes also occur when you are under stress. You may experience changes in your ability to think, such as confusion, trouble concentrating, and inability to remember things or solve problems. You may also experience negative emotions such as fear, anxiety, depression, irritability, anger, and frustration. You may have insomnia or wake up too early and not be able to go back to sleep. It's important to recognize the effects of stress so that you can handle stressful situations before they overwhelm you and affect your ability to perform well in college.

Managing Stress

The best starting point for handling stress is to be in good shape physically and mentally. When your body and mind are healthy, it's like inoculating yourself against stress. This means you need to pay attention to diet, exercise, sleep, relaxation techniques, and other means of relieving stress.

Caffeine and Stress

Your caffeine consumption can have a big impact on your stress level. In moderate amounts (50–200 milligrams per day), caffeine increases alertness and reduces feelings of fatigue. But even at this low intake level, caffeine may make you more energetic during part of the day and more tired later. Consumed in larger quantities, caffeine may cause nervousness, headaches, irritability, stomach irritation, and insomnia—all symptoms of stress. If the amount of caffeine you consume is excessive (this will vary with individuals; watch for symptoms such as inability to sleep and feeling energetic in the morning but tired in the afternoon), replace caffeinated drinks with water or with decaf coffee or tea. Be aware that even a small, five-ounce cup of regular coffee contains 65–115 milligrams of caffeine.

Exercise and Stress

Exercise is an excellent stress management technique, the best way to stay fit, and a critical part of weight loss. While any kind of recreation benefits your body and spirit, aerobic exercise is the best for both stress management and weight control. The American College of Sports Medicine (ACSM) defines aerobic exercise as "any activity that uses large muscle groups, can be maintained continuously, and is rhythmic in nature." It is a type of exercise that gets the heart and lungs to work harder than they work when you are at rest.

© Stockbytet/SuperStock

Intense aerobic activity will help you manage weight and stress.

In aerobic exercise, you work until your pulse is in a target zone, and you keep it in this zone for at least 30 minutes. You can reach your target heart rate through a variety of exercises: for example, walking, jogging, running, swimming, biking, and using a treadmill or stair climber. Choose activities that you enjoy so you will look forward to your exercise time. Also, experts recommend varying what you do so that you don't become bored. If you do these two things, workouts are more likely to become a regular part of your routine.

Besides doing wonders for your body, aerobic exercise also keeps your mind healthy. When you do aerobic exercise, your body produces hormones called beta endorphins. These natural narcotics cause feelings of contentment and happiness and help you to manage anxiety and depression. Your mood and general sense of competence improve with regular aerobic exercise.

Sleep and Stress

Getting adequate sleep is another way to protect yourself from stress. The National Sleep Foundation recommends that adults get eight hours of sleep per night. Lack of sleep can lead to anxiety, depression, and academic problems such as an inability to focus and concentrate. To establish better sleep habits, try these techniques:

- If you can't sleep, get up and do something boring.
- Get your clothes and/or course materials together before you go to bed.
- Avoid long daytime naps.
- Read or listen to a relaxation tape before going to bed.
- Exercise during the day rather than at night.
- Sleep in the same room and bed every night.
- Set a regular schedule for going to bed and getting up.

Relaxation Techniques to Combat Stress

Relaxation techniques such as visualization and deep breathing can help you reduce stress. Learning these skills is just like learning any new skill. You need knowledge and practice. Check your course catalog, college counseling center, health clinic, student newspaper, and fitness center for classes that teach relaxation. You'll find books as well as CDs and DVDs that guide you through relaxation techniques.

Other Ways to Relieve Stress

Here are several other stress relievers you can use to improve your mental health:

- Reward yourself on a regular basis when you achieve small goals.
- Remember that there is a reason you are in a particular situation. Keep the payoff in mind.
- Laugh. A good laugh will almost always make you feel better.
- Pray or meditate.
- Do yoga.
- Practice a hobby.
- Acquire a pet.
- Get a massage.
- Try to clear your mind whenever things get too intense.

Getting Help for Stress

Most campuses have counseling centers that offer one-on-one sessions as well as support groups for their students. Remember that there is no shame attached to being stressed or anxious and that you are not alone in feeling this way. Proper counseling and medical attention when needed can help you deal more effectively with high levels of stress.

Where to Go for Help: Attaining and Maintaining Health and Wellness

Counseling center: Professionals here offer individual and group assistance and lots of information. Their support is nonjudgmental and confidential unless patients are going to harm themselves or others.

Health center/infirmary: On most campuses the professionals who staff these are especially interested in educational outreach and practicing prevention—but treatment is available as well.

Health education and wellness programs: College campuses recognize that for many students, problems

and challenges with alcohol, other drugs, and sexual decision-making and its consequences are part of the college universe. Fellow students who are peer health educators are trained and supervised by professionals and can provide support.

Campus support groups: Many campuses provide student support groups led by professionals, for students dealing with problems related to excessive alcohol and drug use, abusive sexual relationships, and so forth.

Health

Promoting Your Sexual Health

Numerous studies indicate that about 75–80 percent of traditional-age college students have engaged in sexual intercourse at least once.[1] No matter whether you have or haven't had prior sexual experience, it can be helpful to explore your sexual values and to consider whether sex is right for you at this time. If you are having sex and you do not wish to become pregnant or to impregnate someone, you should choose a birth control method and adopt strategies for avoiding sexually transmitted infections (STIs).

Opting for Safer Sex

If you are sexually active, it's important to talk with your partner about ways to protect against sexually transmitted infections and unwanted pregnancy. Communicating with your partner about safer sex can be difficult and even embarrassing initially, but this dialogue can make your relationship stronger and more meaningful.

The most obvious way to avoid STIs and unwanted pregnancy is to not have sex. Celibacy and abstinence are options to consider. For some people, masturbation is a reasonable alternative to sex with a partner.

If you are sexually active, you'll be safer (in terms of STIs) if you have only one partner. Yet you may feel that you're at a point in your life where you would prefer to have multiple relationships simultaneously. Whether you're monogamous or not, you should always protect yourself by using a condom.

In addition to being a contraceptive, a condom can help prevent the spread of STIs. A condom's effectiveness against disease holds true for anal, vaginal, and oral intercourse. The most current research indicates that the rate of protection provided by a condom against STIs is similar to its rate of protection against pregnancy (90–99 percent) when used correctly and consistently for every act of intercourse or oral sex.

Only latex rubber condoms and polyurethane condoms—not lambskin or other types of natural membrane condoms—provide this protection. The polyurethane condom is an excellent alternative for individuals with latex allergies. Use only a water-based lubricant (such as K-Y® Jelly) to keep the condom from breaking.

Practicing Birth Control

What is the best method of contraception? It is any method that you use correctly and consistently each time you have intercourse. Always discuss birth control with your partner so that you both feel comfortable with the option you have selected. For more information about a particular method, consult a pharmacist, your student health center, a local family planning clinic, or your private physician. The important thing is to resolve to protect yourself and your partner every time you have sexual intercourse.

It is important also to know about emergency contraception. What if the condom breaks or you forget to take your birth control pill? Emergency contraceptive pills can reduce the risk of pregnancy from 75 to 89 percent if started within seventy-two hours after unprotected

---

TRY IT! **What's Your Decision?**

Although you might know the strategies to keep yourself from contracting an STI, knowledge doesn't always translate into behavior. List all the reasons you can think of that people wouldn't practice prevention strategies of abstinence, monogamy, or condom use. Then review your list and consider whether each barrier would apply to you ("Yes," "No," or "Maybe"). In this way, you can evaluate where you stand on the issue of safer sex and determine what areas you may need to work on to ensure that you always protect yourself.

---

[1]"National College Health Risk Behavior Study," Centers for Disease Control and Prevention (2005).

vaginal intercourse, according to the Planned Parenthood Federation of America. Most campus health centers and local health clinics dispense emergency contraception to individuals in need.

Avoiding Sexually Transmitted Infections

In recent years epidemic numbers of students on college campuses have become infected with STIs. In general, STIs continue to increase faster than other illnesses on campuses today, and approximately 5 to 10 percent of visits by U.S. college students to college health services are for the diagnosis and treatment of STIs.

STIs are usually spread through genital contact. Sometimes, however, these infections can be transmitted mouth-to-mouth. There are more than twenty known types of STIs; seven are most common on college campuses.

Chlamydia The most common STI in the United States, chlamydia is particularly threatening to women because many show no symptoms. This absence of symptoms can allow the infection to progress to pelvic inflammatory disease (PID), thought to be the main cause of infertility in women.

Human Papilloma Virus (HPV) The leading STI affecting college students, HPV causes warts on the outer genitals and in the rectum of those who practice anal-receptive intercourse. If undetected, HPV can lead to cervical cancer in women. Gardasil, a new vaccine on the market, provides protection against four types of HPV that cause 70 percent of cervical cancer cases. For more information about this vaccine or to receive the three-injection series, contact your college or university health services or local health care provider.

Gonorrhea A bacterial infection with symptoms similar to chlamydia, gonorrhea usually causes pain and burning with urination and possible discharge in men, while women are often asymptomatic.

Herpes The herpes virus affects men and women, and the infection can be both oral and genital. Symptoms include blisters, and currently there is no cure. Infected individuals are most contagious just before or after the blisters erupt.

Hepatitis B Symptoms include yellowing of the skin and eyes and an upset stomach. Some infected people recover completely, while others remain carriers for life. A small percentage will experience permanent liver damage and, in some patients, this disease is fatal. There is no cure or medical treatment for hepatitis B, although it can be prevented with a vaccine.

Hepatitis C Like hepatitis B, hepatitis C is a long-term infection caused by a virus (HCV), but there is no known vaccine for prevention. The disease spreads through blood or bodily fluids and may advance to liver disease.

HIV/AIDS The number of people infected with AIDS and the virus that causes it, HIV, continues to increase. Anyone can contact the disease if exposed to the virus, and heterosexual women are one of the groups at increased risk. Having other STIs may predispose a person to contracting HIV more readily upon exposure.

Practicing abstinence, having only a single partner (one who is uninfected), and using condoms every time you have sex are the best ways to prevent the sexual spread of HIV. For more information, contact your student health service, your local health department, or the National AIDS hotline: 800-342-2437; **http://www.ashastd.org/index.cfm**

Protecting against Sexual Assault

Anyone is at risk for being raped, but the majority of victims are women. By the time they graduate from college, an estimated one out of four college women will be the victim of attempted rape, and one out of six will be raped. Most women will be raped by someone they know—a date or an acquaintance—and most will not report the crime. Alcohol is a factor in nearly three-fourths of the incidents. Whether raped by a date or a stranger, a victim can suffer long-term traumatic effects.

Tricia Phaup of the University of South Carolina offers this advice on avoiding sexual assault:

- Know what you want and do not want sexually.
- Go to social gatherings with friends, and leave with them.
- Avoid being alone with people you don't know very well.
- Trust your intuition.
- Be alert to subtle and unconscious messages you may be sending and receiving.
- Be aware of how much alcohol you drink, if any.

If you are ever tempted to force another person to have sex:

- Realize that it is never okay to force sex on someone.
- Don't assume that you know what your date wants.
- If you're getting mixed messages, ask.
- Be aware of the effects of alcohol.
- Remember that rape is morally and legally wrong.

If you have been raped, regardless of whether you choose to report the rape to the police or get a medical exam, it is very helpful to seek counseling by contacting resources such as a campus sexual assault coordinator, local rape crisis center, campus police department, student health services, women's student services, local hospital emergency rooms, and campus chaplains.

Making Decisions about Drinking and Smoking

Even if you don't drink, the information in this section is important, because 50 percent of college students reported helping a drunken friend, classmate, or study partner in the past year. This information could improve, or even save, your life or the life of someone you care about.

Alcohol can turn people into victims even though they don't drink—for example, people who are killed by drunk drivers, and family members who suffer from the behavior of an alcoholic. Over the course of one year, about 20 to 30 percent of students report serious problems related to excessive alcohol use. You may have heard news reports about college students who died or were seriously or permanently injured as a result of excessive drinking. Just one occasion of heavy or high-risk drinking can lead to problems.

Alcohol abuse is a serious problem among college students. Why do you think this is true?

Drinking and Blood Alcohol Content

How alcohol affects behavior depends on the dose of alcohol, which is best measured by blood alcohol content, or BAC. Most of the pleasurable effects of alcoholic beverages are experienced at lower BAC levels, when alcohol acts as a behavioral stimulant. For most people, the stimulant level is around one drink per hour. Usually, problems begin at an intake higher than .05, when alcohol acts as a sedative and starts to slow down areas of the brain. Most people who have more than four or five drinks at one occasion feel "buzzed," show signs of impairment, and are likely to be at higher risk for alcohol-related problems. However, significant impairment at lower doses can occur.

How fast you drink makes a difference, too. Your body gets rid of alcohol at a rate of about one drink an hour. Drinking more than one drink an hour may cause a rise in BAC because the body is absorbing alcohol faster than it can eliminate it.

Alcohol and Behavior

At BAC levels of .025 to .05, a drinker tends to feel animated and energized. At a BAC level of around .05, a drinker may feel rowdy or boisterous. This is the point where most people report feeling a buzz from alcohol. At a BAC level between .05 and .08, alcohol starts to act as a depressant. When people start to feel that buzz, they are on the brink of losing coordination, clear thinking, and judgment.

Driving is measurably impaired even at BAC levels lower than the legal limit of .08. An accurate safe level for most people may be half the legal limit (.04). As BAC levels climb past .08, people become progressively less coordinated and less able to make good decisions. Most with BAC levels higher than .08 become severely uncoordinated and may drift into sleep, fall down, or slur their speech.

Recognizing Warning Signs and Saving Lives

Most people pass out or fall asleep when their BAC is above .25. Unfortunately, even after you pass out and stop drinking, your BAC can continue to rise as alcohol in your stomach is released to the intestine and absorbed into the bloodstream. Your body may try to get rid of alcohol by vomiting, but you can choke if you are unconscious, semiconscious, or severely uncoordinated.

Worse yet, at BAC levels higher than .30, most people will show signs of severe alcohol poisoning, such as an inability to wake up, slowed breathing, fast but

Health

weak pulse, cool or damp skin, and pale or bluish skin. Anyone exhibiting these symptoms needs medical assistance immediately. If you find someone in such a state, keep the person on her side with the head lower than the rest of the body. Check to see that the airway is clear, especially if the person is vomiting or if the tongue is blocking the back of the throat.

Heavy Drinking: The Danger Zone

Research suggests that light to moderate drinking has some risks, but heavy drinking is associated with a substantially elevated risk of alcohol-related problems. Heavy drinking, sometimes called binge drinking, is commonly defined as five or more drinks for males and four or more drinks for females on a single occasion. Presumably, for a very large person who drinks slowly over a long period of time (several hours), four or five drinks may not lead to a BAC associated with impairment. However, research suggests that in many cases the BAC of heavy drinkers exceeds the legal limit for impairment (.08).

The academic, medical, and social consequences of heavy drinking can seriously endanger the quality of life. Research based on surveys conducted by the Core Institute at Southern Illinois University (**http://www.siu.edu/departments/coreinst/public_html/**) provides substantial evidence that heavy drinkers, as compared with all drinkers and all students, have a significantly greater risk of adverse outcomes, including increased risk of poor test performance, missed classes, unlawful behavior, violence, memory loss, drunk driving, regretful behavior, and vandalism. At the same time, college health centers nationwide are reporting increasing occurrences of serious medical conditions—even death—resulting from excessive alcohol use. These medical problems include alcohol poisoning, leading to coma and shock; respiratory depression, choking, and respiratory arrest; head trauma and brain injury; lacerations and fractures; and unwanted or unsafe sexual activity causing STIs and pregnancies.

If you engage in heavy drinking so long that your body can tolerate large amounts of alcohol, you may become an alcoholic. Fortunately, most college students do not advance to alcoholism. However, if you or someone you know shows signs of becoming an alcoholic, you should contact a source on campus that can help. The student health center is a good starting place, but an instructor, a minister, or an academic adviser can also counsel you on where to seek help.

Tobacco—The Other Legal Drug

Tobacco use is clearly the cause of many serious medical conditions, including heart disease, cancer, and lung ailments. Over the years, tobacco has led to the

TRY IT! Sharing and Comparing Experiences

List five ways your or a friend's quality of life has been influenced by others' drinking or smoking. In small groups, share some or all of these with others. What did you find out when you compared your experiences with theirs? Did you handle the situation in a healthy manner in comparison to other members of your group? What would you do differently in the future?

deaths of hundreds of thousands of individuals, and, unfortunately, many college students smoke. The College Tobacco Prevention Resource estimates that approximately 30 percent of college students are current users, meaning they have used a tobacco product in the past thirty days. However, the greatest concern about college students and tobacco usage is social smoking—smoking only when hanging out with friends, drinking, or partying.

The Centers for Disease Control report that among eighteen- to twenty-four-year-old college students, 28.7 percent fall into the social smoker category.[2] Most college students who smoke socially feel they will be able to give up their smoking habits once they graduate—but after four years of college, many find that they are addicted to cigarettes. A national tobacco study reported that almost 40 percent of college students either began smoking or became regular smokers after starting college.[3]

Chemicals in tobacco are so highly addictive that they make it hard to quit. Although young people may not worry about long-term side effects such as lung cancer and emphysema, increased numbers of respiratory infections, worsening of asthma, bad breath, stained teeth, and the huge expense should be motivations to not start smoking at all. Many institutions and local hospitals offer smoking cessation programs to help individuals addicted to nicotine quit smoking. If you smoke, contact your campus health center for more information about how to quit.

[2]CDC, "Prevalence of Current Cigarette Smoking among Adults and Change in Prevalence of Current and Some Day Smoking—United States, 1996–2000," *Morbidity and Mortality Weekly Report 52*, no. 14 (April 2003): 303–307.

[3]N. Rigotti, J. Lee, and H. Wechsler, "U.S. College Students' Use of Tobacco Products: Results of a National Survey," *Journal of the American Medical Association 284*, no. 6 (2000): 699–705.

Health

Saying No to Drug Abuse

The abuse of prescription drugs is a growing problem on campuses. Researchers at the University of Michigan reported in January 2005 that 7 percent of college students have used prescription stimulants for nonmedical purposes at some point and 4 percent have used them in the past year. College students' nonmedical use of prescription pain relievers is increasing. Some individuals may "doctor shop" to get multiple prescriptions for the drugs they abuse.

Illegal recreational drugs such as marijuana, cocaine, methamphetamine, Ecstasy, and heroin are used by a much smaller number of college students and far less frequently than alcohol. Yet these drugs, too, pose significant health issues for college students. The penalties associated with the possession or abuse of illegal drugs tend to be much more severe than those associated with underage alcohol use.

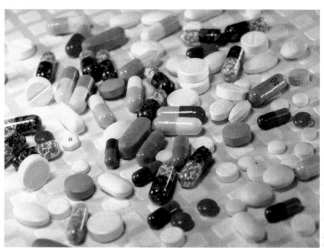

© Steve Allen/Getty Images

Prescription Drug Abuse

Three classes of prescription drugs are the most commonly abused: opioids, central nervous system (CNS) depressants, and stimulants. Abuse of anabolic steroids is also on the rise. Athletic departments, potential employers, and government agencies routinely screen for abuse of prescription drugs.

Opioids Opioids include morphine, codeine, and such branded drugs as OxyContin, Darvon, Vicodin, Demerol, and Dilaudid. Opioids work by blocking the transmission of pain messages to the brain. Chronic use can result in addiction. Taking a large single dose of an opioid can cause a severe reduction in your breathing rate that can lead to death.

CNS depressants Taken under a doctor's care, central nervous system (CNS) depressants can be useful in the treatment of anxiety and sleep disorders. The flip side is that exceeding the recommended dosage can create a tolerance, and the user will need larger doses to achieve the same result. If the user stops taking the drug, the brain's activity can rebound and race out of control, possibly leading to seizures and other harmful consequences.

Stimulants Stimulants such as ephedrine, Ritalin, and Dexadrine enhance brain activity, causing an increase in alertness, attention, and energy accompanied by elevated blood pressure and increased heart rate.

Legal use of stimulants to treat obesity, asthma, and other problems has dropped off as their potential for abuse and addiction has become apparent.[4]

Ritalin is prescribed for a condition called ADHD (attention deficit hyperactivity disorder) but has gained recognition on college campuses as a "cramming drug." This prescription drug costs only about fifty cents per tablet but sells on the street for as much as fifteen dollars. College students are using Ritalin to stay awake for long periods of time to study for exams. Many students think that because it is a prescribed drug, Ritalin must be harmless. But the fact is that abusing Ritalin can cause nervousness, vomiting, changes in heart rate and blood pressure, dependency, fevers, convulsions, headaches, paranoia, hallucinations, and delusions.

Anabolic steroids When most people think of steroids, they think about college and professional athletes who use these manufactured substances to build their strength and improve their athletic performance. But it is important for all college students to know and understand the dangers of steroids.

According to the National Institute on Drug Abuse, steroids are taken orally or injected into the body in cycles lasting weeks or months. Steroid abuse has many major side effects, including liver tumors, cancer, jaundice, fluid retention, high blood pressure, kidney tumors,

---

[4]Adapted from "Prescription Drugs: Abuse and Addiction," National Institute on Drug Abuse, part of the National Institutes of Health (NIH), a division of the U.S. Department of Health and Human Services (DHHS) (2001).

Health

and severe acne. Most anabolic steroid users are male and therefore have gender-specific side effects including shrinking of the testicles, reduced sperm count, infertility, baldness, development of breasts, and increased risk for prostate cancer. Abusers also put themselves at risk for contracting HIV or other blood-borne viruses when using or sharing infected needles.

The abuse rate for steroids is fairly low among the general population. In 2003, the "Monitoring the Future Survey" found that 1.8 percent of young adults aged nineteen to twenty-eight reported using steroids at least once during their lifetimes. One-half (0.5) percent reported using steroids at least once in the past year, and 0.2 percent reported using steroids in the past month.[5]

Illegal Drugs

Athletic departments, potential employers, and government agencies routinely screen for many commonly used illegal drugs. Future employability, athletic scholarships, and insurability may be compromised if you have a positive drug test for any of these substances.

Marijuana Marijuana has an effect on the body and its functions for three to seven days, depending on the potency and the smoker. Like alcohol, light use will produce a high. But chronic usage of marijuana can lead to a lethargic state in which users may forget about current responsibilities (such as going to class). Long-term use carries the same risks of lung infections and cancer that are associated with smoking tobacco.

Ecstasy MDMA, or Ecstasy, as it is known, is a synthetic, or manufactured, drug. While many young people believe that MDMA is safe and offers nothing but a pleasant high for the twenty-five dollar cost of a single tablet, the reality is far different. Taken orally, MDMA produces effects that last approximately four to six hours. Many abusers will take a second dose when the initial dose begins to fade. Some Ecstasy tablets contain not only MDMA but also other drugs, including amphetamine, caffeine, destromethorpin, ephedrine, and cocaine.

MDMA significantly depletes serotonin, a substance in the brain that helps regulate mood, sleep, pain, emotion, appetite, and other behaviors. It takes the brain time to rebuild the serotonin needed to perform important physiological and psychological functions. Of great concern are MDMA's adverse effects on the pumping efficiency of the heart. Heavy users may experience obsessive traits, anxiety, paranoia, and sleep

disturbance. Another study indicates that MDMA can have long-lasting effects on memory.[6]

Heroin Numerous reports have suggested a rise in heroin use among college students. A highly addictive drug with the potential to be more damaging and fatal than other opiates, heroin is the most abused and most rapidly acting of this group. One of the most significant—and surest—effects of heroin use is addiction. The human body begins to develop tolerance to the drug on first use. Once this happens, the abuser must use more of the drug to achieve a high of the same intensity.

Heroin can be injected, smoked, or snorted. Injection is the most efficient way to administer low-purity heroin. However, the availability of high-purity heroin and the fear of infection by sharing needles have made snorting and smoking the drug more common. Some users believe that snorting or smoking heroin will not lead to addiction. They are 100 percent wrong.

Chronic users may develop collapsed veins, infection of the heart lining and valves, abscesses, and liver disease. In addition, users are at risk for pulmonary complications, including various types of pneumonia. Beyond the effects of the drug itself, users who inject heroin or share needles also put themselves at risk for contracting HIV, hepatitis B and C, and other blood-borne viruses.

Cocaine Cocaine or crack produces an intense experience that heightens senses. A crack high lasts only a few minutes; then the good feelings are gone. During the crash, the user may feel tired and unmotivated and find it impossible to sleep. Cocaine is highly addictive. In some instances, users have died of cardiac arrest while taking the drug.

Meth (methamphetamine) Methamphetamine is particularly dangerous because it costs so little, is so easy to make, and is therefore more available to users. Much of it is produced in makeshift labs in homes or college residences, and so its quality varies from batch to batch and it's impossible to tell what else is in the mixture. The drug can initially produce euphoria, enhanced wakefulness, increased physical activity, and decreased appetite. Prolonged use can lead to binges, during which users take more meth every few hours for several days until they run out or become too disorganized to continue. Chronic abuse can lead to psychotic behavior, characterized by intense paranoia, visual and auditory hallucinations, and out-of-control rages that can be coupled with extremely violent behavior.

[5]"2004 Monitoring the Future Survey," funded by the National Institute on Drug Abuse, NIH (DHHS) and conducted by the University of Michigan's Institute for Social Research. For more data, go online at **www.drugabuse.gov**.

[6]Excerpted from "Ecstasy: What We Know and Don't Know About MDMA: A Scientific Review." National Institute on Drug Abuse, part of the NIH, a division of the DHHS (2004).

Health

WIRED WINDOW

IT'S CALLED "INTERNET ADDICTION" and researchers have discovered that problems arising from Internet use have more to do with *how people use* rather than *how much time they spend on* the Internet. College students who use the Internet for communicating with others are less likely to be addicted than those who use the Internet for shopping, reading news, and checking sports scores. Communicating via the Internet might allow introverted students to make friends more easily. Students who are more engaged in their studies and in campus life tend to be more successful in college. Yet students who use the Internet extensively tend to have less time for real-world social contacts. How do you use the Internet? For this week, keep a record of how much time you spend online and how much time you spend on each of the following activities: Instant Messaging, Facebook, MySpace, email, reading news, shopping, checking sports scores, playing multiplayer games, and/or playing single-player games. How much time did you spend online? How did you spend most of your time online? If you found that you are online more for shopping, reading news, checking sports scores, and/or playing single-player games, do you have strong relationships with friends outside of the wired world? If you didn't like what you discovered, you might want to talk to a counselor at your college to help you manage your Internet activities.

▶▶▶ BUILDING YOUR PORTFOLIO

Are You "Technostressed"?

Imagine if every Thursday your shoes exploded if you tied them the usual way.
This happens to us all the time with computers, and nobody thinks of complaining.

–Jef Raskin (1943–2005), American human-computer interface expert

Ever-changing, ever-improving technology is a wonderful part of our modern world, but it can also be an additional stressor on our everyday lives. It seems the list of hot new gadgets grows longer every day. How does being a constantly accessible, multitasking marvel with continuous reminders of what you haven't done yet affect your stress level? Do you occasionally find yourself overwhelmed or even a bit lonely when you are face-to-face with your computer instead of your friends, families, or coworkers? The hurried, plugged-in life can be exhausting and nerve-racking, especially if you get an incomprehensible error message on your computer screen the night before a big paper is due!

So, how are you plugged in?

1. Create a new entry in your portfolio with the title "Technostressed." Record your work for this assignment there.

2. Describe all the ways your life is affected by technology. How are your health and well-being affected, both positively and negatively, by the things you list?

   Tip: Think of how you use technology for entertainment, and also for class or work.

Sometimes it seems like all of the technology that is supposed to make our lives easier actually adds to the balancing act. Here are a few tips for reducing your stress level and avoiding a technology takeover.

- Schedule some downtime offline for yourself.
- Don't become a text-message junkie.
- Don't try to multitask 24/7! Take advantage of time to exercise, eat, or just take a break without the demands of email and cell phones.

Recognize the warning signs of Internet addiction, such as the following:

- Using the Internet to escape from problems or responsibilities
- Missing class, work, or appointments to spend time online
- Always allowing the Internet to substitute for face-to-face interaction with others

Experiencing College Life to the Fullest:

Getting Involved on Campus and in the Wider Community

© Mark Richards/PhotoEdit

Going to college means far more than attending classes and labs, studying, taking tests, and writing papers. For many students, the college experience also means volunteering in the community, joining a club or an organization, or working at a job.

Are you involved in activities beyond your academic work? The college environment presents a world of out-of-classroom opportunities that allow you to develop friendships; to grow intellectually, socially, and culturally; and to experience campus diversity.

Do you have a job on or off campus? If so, do you work part time, or are you a returning or continuing education student with a full-time job? College presents unique opportunities for learning about the world of work or about industries and professions firsthand. If you want to balance your academic studies with on-site hands-on learning, then internships, co-op programs, and service learning are some of the options that may be available to you.

Balancing the demands of courses, out-of-class activities, jobs, and careers (and often family obligations, too) can be challenging. But learning how to manage your responsibilities and obligations is essential to college success. ■

Service activities provide a great way to meet different people and to help others.

In this step you will learn:

- how to find a job if you must work during college

- what the advantages and disadvantages of working during college are

- why working on campus is preferable to taking a job off campus

- how being active in campus organizations and groups can benefit you

- what to know about joining campus groups

- what internships and co-op programs are and how they can benefit you

- how you can embrace, learn from, and work in support of campus diversity

- how you can use service learning to clarify your values, develop your skills, and participate in activities to improve your community, your region, and your country

How Do You Measure Up?

Experiencing College Life to the Fullest

Check the following items that apply to you:

_____ 1. I have looked into the various organizations and groups on my campus, and I have explored joining one or more.

_____ 2. I understand the advantages and the disadvantages of belonging to a Greek social organization.

_____ 3. I recognize the ways that joining a club or a group affiliated with my major or reflecting my career interests can enhance my career options.

_____ 4. I have grappled honestly with the question of whether I truly need to work while attending college.

_____ 5. If I must work, I understand the benefits of working on campus versus off campus.

_____ 6. I have checked campus resources to find out about community service opportunities.

_____ 7. I understand the career benefits of internships and co-op programs.

_____ 8. I take advantage of the special opportunities the campus provides me to interact with a wide range of people from different cultures, ages, and life experiences.

_____ 9. I have participated in campus efforts to promote multiculturalism and diversity.

_____ 10. I understand what service learning entails and how it differs from other kinds of community service.

Review the items you did not check. Paying attention to all these aspects of your college experience can be very important to your success. After reading this step, come back to this list and choose an item or two that you did not check but are willing to work on.

Philip Gardner, Michigan State University; Tom Carskadon, Mississippi State University; Juan Flores, Folsom Lake College; and Edward Zlotkowski, Bentley College contributed their valuable and considerable expertise to the writing of this section.

Being Active in Campus and Community Life

Colleges and universities can seem huge and unfriendly, especially if you went to a small high school or grew up in a small town. Whether you are attending a school close to home or farther away, and whether you are living at home or on your own for the first time, the adjustment may be overwhelming. To feel comfortable in your new environment, you need to find your comfort zone or niche. Many students discover that becoming involved in campus organizations eases the transition. They also find that it helps them make connections with other students, faculty, and staff members and prepares them for the world of work.

It's not hard to find a place where you belong, but it will take some initiative. Consider your interests and the activities that you enjoy most, and explore opportunities related to them. You might be interested in joining an intramural team, performing community service, running for a student government office, or getting involved in the residence hall. Or you might prefer joining a more structured club or organization that has chapters on many campuses. Campus organizations can be recreational; your school may have a rock climbing club, billiards league, and/or a glee club, for example. You'll find others that are more academically and career oriented, such as the Spanish Club, the Electrical Engineering Society, and the Student Nurses' Association. And many campuses have

groups that provide resources and social outlets for students in similar situations (for example, Students with Children, and the International Students' Association).

To find the organization that's right for you, check out campus newspapers, activity fairs, printed guides, open houses, and web pages. Many campuses also have a student activities office located in a central facility, often called the student union, for student clubs and programs. And your first-year seminar instructor may spend time in class describing different clubs and organizations and talking about the overall benefits of campus involvement. If you become interested in a certain group or activity, consider attending a meeting before you make the decision to join. See what the organization is like, what the expectations of time and money are, and whether you feel comfortable with the members. As you explore your options, consider that new students who become involved with at least one organization are more likely to be successful in their first year and remain in college.

Your campus is part of a larger community. If you live on campus, find a way to learn more about the community around you. Even if this community is your hometown, you will learn much about it that is new when you experience the community with a fresh eye. Some campuses offer students the opportunity to interact with a community mentor—an older individual who may or may not be an alumnus of the institution and who can help you find things to do, places to go, and people to meet in the local area. Consider participating in a community service project. Your college may offer service opportunities as part of first-year courses (service learning—see pp. 132-133), or your campus's division of student affairs may have a volunteer or community service office.

Joining On-Campus Groups

Is Greek life right for you? Some, but not all, colleges and universities are the home for Greek organizations, commonly called fraternities or sororities, that are social groups for men and women known by their Greek letter names. Fraternities and sororities can be a

© Chris Nash/Getty Images

rich source of friends and support, and some students love them. But other students may not think a Greek organization is the right fit for them and may choose not to participate in one.

Fraternities and sororities provide a quick connection to a large number of individuals on your campus and beyond—a link to a social network, camaraderie, and support. Some campuses have several fraternities and sororities to choose from, each differing in philosophy and image. There are even fraternities and sororities created by and for specific racial or ethnic groups. These have existed for a number of years and were established by students of color who felt the need for campus groups that allowed them to connect to their community and culture while in school. Nu Alpha Kappa Fraternity, Alpha Rho Lambda Sorority, Omega Psi Phi Fraternity, Alpha Kappa Alpha Sorority, Lamba Phi Epsilon Fraternity, and Sigma Omicron Pi Sorority are just a few of the many ethnically based Greek organizations that exist across the country. Such organizations have provided many students with a means to become familiar with their campus and to gain friendship and support, while promoting their culture and ethnicity.

Fraternities and sororities are powerful social influences, so you'll definitely want to take a good look at the sophomores, juniors, and seniors in them. If what you see is what you want to be and if you are willing to pay the fees and recurring membership dues, consider joining. But if you decide that Greek life is not for you, there are many other great ways to make close friends.

Career/major organizations

You might also find your niche on campus by taking part in activities that reflect your major and career interests. Belonging to an organization that focuses on a specific field of study can provide a well-rounded college experience and also can be a great asset in your future or current career. Join a club that is affiliated with your major or reflects your career interest. Becoming a member will not only help you find out more about your field of interest but also allow you to make contacts that can enhance your career options. Many campus clubs participate in challenges and contests with similar groups from other colleges and contribute to campus activities through exhibitions and events. The Psychology Club; the Math, Engineering, and Science Association; and the Association of Student Filmmakers are examples of groups dedicated to specific academic fields.

TRY IT! Finding Your Niche on Campus

Search your school's web page for information on campus organizations and groups. Which ones dovetail with some of your present interests and talents? Which ones focus on activities and programs that are new to you but that you are interested in exploring? List the groups and organizations that catch your attention, along with the contact information for each, and take steps to learn more about them.

Political/activist organizations

You may also want to get involved on campus by joining a politically active group. Campuses are home to many organizations that are dedicated to specific political affiliations and causes. Campus Republicans, Young Democrats, Amnesty International, Native Students in Social Action, and other groups provide students with a platform to express their political views and share their causes with others. These organizations typically host debating events and forums to address current issues and events.

Special-interest groups

Perhaps the largest subgroup of student clubs is the special-interest category, which comprises everything from recreational interests to hobbies. On your campus you may find special-interest organizations as varied as the Brazilian Jujitsu Club, the Kite Flyers' Club, the Flamenco Club, and the Video Gamers' Society. Students can cultivate an interest in bird watching or indulge their curiosity about ballroom dance without ever leaving campus. Many of these clubs sponsor campus events highlighting their specific interests and talents; these occasions provide an ideal way to learn about the organizations. Check out the ones you're most curious about. If a club is not available, create it yourself and contribute to the social opportunities on your campus!

Becoming involved—on or off campus, or both—helps you gain valuable knowledge, broaden your exposure to new ideas, make useful contacts, and develop a support network. You'll find that time spent in these outside-of-class endeavors can be just as important as the time inside your classes. Remember: not all learning occurs in the classroom. Participating enriches your time in college and connects you to the wider campus and the external community.

Community

Working While in College

It's a fact that most students work, and there are pluses and minuses to working in college. Work can support you in attaining your college goals, provide you with the financial means to complete college, and help you structure your time so that you are a much better time manager. It can help you meet people who will later serve as important references for graduate school and/or employment. But working too much can interfere with your college experience and your academic success. It can get in the way of attending class, doing homework, and participating in many other valuable college pursuits, such as group activities, foreign study, and travel.

If you feel that you have to work in order to pay for your tuition and/or your living expenses, take time to determine honestly how much you need to work, and stay within reasonable limits. Many college students work too many hours just to support a lifestyle—to buy or maintain a brand-new car; to purchase designer clothes or that MP3 player they've had their eye on. It's important to keep a reasonable balance between work and study. Don't fall into the trap of thinking "I can do it all." Too many college students have found that "doing it all" means they don't do anything very well.

Working on Campus

If you want to work, try to find a job on campus. Even if a campus job pays less than you could earn off campus, there are real advantages to on-campus employment. Generally, your on-campus supervisors will be much more flexible than off-campus employers in helping you balance your study demands and your work schedule. And the relationships you'll develop with influential people who really care about your success in college and who will write those all-important reference letters will make the smaller paycheck well worth it.

Your career center can tell you how to get information about college employment. You may have to register in person or online, but the process is easy, especially if you have a résumé or a draft of one. College employment systems generally channel all jobs collected through faculty, advisers, and career counselors into one database, so it is convenient for you to identify jobs that are right for you.

Many campuses offer an on-campus job fair during the first weeks of the fall term. Even if you might not be interested at the time, stopping by the job fair will give you a great idea of the range and type of jobs available on campus. You will be pleasantly surprised to learn that there are more opportunities for on-campus work than washing dishes in the cafeteria. Usually job fairs also include off-campus community employers, in part because your institution must spend some of the federal college work-study funds it receives supporting off-campus work by students.

It is a good idea to pursue job opportunities that are related to your major or your career. For example, if you are a pre-med major, you might be able to find on-campus work in a biology or chemistry lab. That work would help you to gain knowledge and experience and to make connections with faculty experts in these fields. In fact, getting an on-campus job is one of the best ways to develop relationships with instructors and administrators on your campus.

Working off Campus

If you decide to work off campus, try to find a job that relates to your academic interests. Also seek a job that will provide you the flexibility you will need to meet

If you're a pre-med in need of a job, check out opportunities in campus biology and chemistry labs.

Community

College Jobs and Your Career

At this point in your college experience, you probably have at least tentative plans about the major and/or the career you will pursue. If you must take a job while going to school, think about what jobs may be available on campus and in the outside community that might provide valuable experience with respect to your goals. Make two lists—one for on-campus jobs and the other for off-campus jobs—that identify jobs related to your career interests, and look into the availability of such work.

your college obligations. You don't want to find yourself caught in the middle of your employer's and your professors' expectations if you can avoid it. If you opt for an off-campus job, the best places to start looking are your campus career center and/or your financial aid office. Check out various resources such as listings or websites with off-campus employment opportunities. Don't hesitate to speak to a career counselor for suggestions. You may also want to consider internship opportunities or co-op programs, if your campus provides this option.

Internships

Your academic department or the campus career center can provide information on off-campus internships that may be available. Internships offer valuable hands-on experience in a career you may want to pursue. Through an internship, you'll learn not only about the nature of the industry and the daily work routine but also about employment in an organization. You'll work with people who can be instrumental in helping you find a job when your studies are done. And adding the experience of having been an intern to your résumé will make it all the stronger when the time comes for a job search.

Co-op Programs

Some colleges and universities have "co-op programs," in which you spend some terms in class and other terms in temporary job settings in your field. Although they usually prolong your education somewhat, co-op programs have many advantages. They offer an excellent preview of what work in your chosen field is like and give you valuable experience and contacts that you can tap into to get a job when you finish college; in fact, many firms offer successful co-op students permanent jobs when they graduate. Alternating work and school terms may be a more agreeable schedule for you than eight or ten straight terms of classes would be, and the work/academics balance may help you keep your ultimate goal in mind. Co-op programs can help you pay for college, too; during their co-op terms, some co-op

students, especially in technical fields, make almost as much as their professors do!

Here are some other suggestions for locating off-campus work:

- Learn the names of the major employers in your college's geographic area: manufacturers, service industries, resorts, and so on. For example, some campuses are near UPS distribution centers, which are well-known for favoring college students for lucrative part-time union-wage-scale jobs. Once you identify the major local employers, check them out, visit their websites, and learn more.
- Every state in the country has a state agency to collect and disseminate information about available employment opportunities. Check out the relevant website and see if your state agency has an office in the community where you are attending college.
- Visit employment agencies, particularly those that seek part-time temporary workers. This is a convenient, low-risk (for both you and the employer) way to shop for a job and to obtain flexible, short-term, low-commitment employment.
- Visit online job boards, and look at the classified ads in the local newspaper, in print, or online. And don't forget the classifieds in the national press. Some national firms will have jobs that can be done part-time in your area or even from your own living space.
- Read your campus newspaper to get leads. Employers who favor hiring college students advertise in campus newspapers.
- Most jobs are never posted, so network with your professors, other students, and campus employees to see if they know of an opportunity that may be right for you. Employers find it easier to hire people recommended to them by current employees, friends, or the person vacating the position. Faculty members often hire students for their research labs on the basis of performance in the classroom.
- Your personal connections are important, so maintain them and let your friends know that you are looking for a job. Your friends who already work on campus or who have had an internship may be the best people to help you when you are ready to search for your job. Amazing as it sounds, nearly 50 percent of all jobs are found through family and friends.

The bottom line is to try to limit the number of hours you work while you're in college. Research finds that students who work more than fifteen or twenty hours a week have a lower chance of finishing college. And students who work off campus, as opposed to on campus, are also less likely to be successful in college unless their work is directly connected with their major.

Embracing Campus Diversity

Getting involved in college life outside the classroom is a terrific opportunity to meet and learn from new and different individuals. At this point in your college experience, you are surely aware of the diversity of the student body on your campus. Your campus provides you a unique opportunity to interact with, and learn along with, a kaleidoscope of individuals—people with a range of religious affiliations, sexual orientations, ethnicities, ages, cultures, and abilities.

Student-run organizations can provide you with multiple avenues to express ideas, pursue interests, and cultivate relationships with those who are different from you. All student-run organizations are in fact culturally based and provide an outlet for the promotion and celebration of that culture. Take, for instance, two very different student groups—let's call them the "Muslim Student Union" and the "Animation Club"—and apply the components of culture to them. Both groups promote a belief system that is common among their members. The first is based on religious beliefs, and the second on what constitutes animation as an art form. Both have aspects that can be taught and passed on: on the one hand, the teachings and practices of the Muslim faith; and on the other hand, the rules and techniques applied in drawing. Both use language specific to their members. Many campus organizations and clubs such as these bring like-minded students together and are open to anyone who wants to become involved.

Colleges and universities promote multicultural learning and discovery not only inside the classroom but outside as well. They sponsor programs that highlight ethnic and cultural celebrations such as Chinese New Year and Kwanzaa; that explore topics of gender such as Taking Back the Night; and that bring in a broad range of entertainment, including concerts, lectures, and art exhibits. By taking part in these events, you will gain exposure to new and exciting ideas and viewpoints and enhance your education.

Helping to Make Campus Diversity Thrive

Some students get involved in campus life by joining with others to cultivate and preserve campus diversity. In addition to sponsoring various cultural programs and special events, these groups work to foster an atmosphere where different heritages, life experiences,

Campuses provide virtually unlimited opportunities to experience diversity.

© Kate M. Deioma/PhotoEdit

Community

and views count. When the activities or free expression of any group is threatened, its members might form action committees and will make it clear that prejudice and hate crimes—any prejudicial activity, including physical assault, vandalism, intimidation, and graffiti that expresses racial, ethnic, or cultural slurs—will not be ignored or tolerated.

What can you do to promote and protect diversity? First, you can work with existing campus services such as the campus police, campus chaplains, or the diversity or multicultural center, as well as with faculty and the administration, to plan and host educational opportunities such as training, workshops, and symposiums on diversity, sensitivity, and multiculturalism. You also can take part in antidiscrimination events on campus, in which campus and community leaders address the issues and provide solutions. You can join prevention programs to devise strategies to battle hate crimes on campus or in the community. In addition, you can look into what antidiscriminatory measures the college is employing, and consider whether they need updating or revision.

Challenge yourself to become involved in making your campus a safe place in which students with diverse views, lifestyles, languages, politics, religions, and interests can come together and be educated. Your education will be richer, and your training to be a successful contributor to the global economy will be stronger, if they develop in an atmosphere that values diversity. Indeed, the inclusiveness of campus culture will give you a competitive advantage as you make your way in life.

Where to Go for Help

On Campus

The majority of colleges and university campuses have taken an active role in promoting diversity on their campuses. In the effort to ensure a welcoming and supportive environment for all students, institutions have established offices, centers, and resources with the intent of providing students with educational opportunities, academic guidance, and support networks. Look into the availability of the following resources on your campus, and visit one or more:

Office of Student Affairs
Office of Diversity
Multicultural Centers
Women's and Men's Centers
Gay, Lesbian, and Bisexual, and Transgendered
  Student Alliances
Centers for Students with Disabilities
Academic support programs for
  under-represented groups

Online

The Riley Guide: http://www.rileyguide.com. One of the best sites for interviewing, job search strategies, and other critical career tips.

Mapping Your Future: http://www.mapping yourfuture.org. This comprehensive site provides support for those who are just starting to explore careers.

Student Now Diversity Resources: http://www .studentnow.com/collegelist/diversity.html. A list of campus diversity resources.

Reaping the Benefits of Service Learning

"**S**ervice learning" is an educational method that combines meaningful service to the community with curriculum-based learning. Service learning has several specific aspects:

■ **Serving** The service itself should address a genuine community need, as determined by existing or student-led community assessments. The service should be thoughtfully organized to solve, or to make a positive contribution toward solving, a problem.

■ **Linking** In quality service learning, the service project is designed to meet not only a real community need but also classroom goals. By ensuring strong linkages between the service and the learning, students are able to improve their academic skills and apply what they learn in school to the broader community and vice versa.

■ **Learning Reflection** Careful thought, especially the process of reconsidering previous actions, events, and decisions is a key element of service learning. The instructor structures time and methods for students to reflect on their service experience.

Service learning is both related to and yet different from two other kinds of off-campus activities with which you may be familiar: community service and internships. Like community service, service learning seeks to help others, to contribute to the common good. Indeed, students involved in service learning and in community service often work at the same community site.

But there are also important differences, such as service learning's emphasis on reflection and reciprocity (something done mutually or in return). Although a student may learn a lot through traditional community service, service learning does not leave such learning to chance. Instead, it surrounds the service experience with carefully designed reflection activities to help students prepare for, process, and pull together different aspects of their experience. Because reflection and reciprocity require a formal structure to make them effective, service learning often takes place in and through specially designed academic courses.

Let's look at some reasons why more and more students are making service learning an important part of their education.

Using Service Learning to Clarify Values

There is probably no better way for you to clarify what you really value than to put yourself in a situation where your assumptions and beliefs are tested. Suppose you've always assumed you wanted to be an accountant. You take a course with a service-learning requirement that asks you to reconcile the books at a local nonprofit organization. You set about putting some method in their madness—and you hate it! Or suppose you've always believed you wanted to be a teacher, and your service-learning assignment is to teach a group of immigrant fourth-grade students how to read in English. You may find that you are able to teach these students effectively, or you may discover that you simply don't have the patience that such a job requires. In either case, you may find your untested beliefs about what you value in a work situation challenged by reality. And as a result of your experience, you've now got some important additional information to use in making a career choice.

Identifying Value Dualisms

"Value dualisms" are conflicts between different things someone professes to believe. Service learning is one of the most powerful tools we have to bring such conflicts to consciousness. In other words, immersion in service learning helps individuals better understand their personal value systems and the strength of their stated beliefs.

Although most students find the very experience of being on a campus a good opportunity to reexamine personal values, it's also true that most of us quickly seek out others more or less similar to us. Service learning helps to ensure that your college years really do teach you to stretch and to move outside your comfort zone.

Developing Skills

Still another set of benefits associated with service learning has to do with skills and competencies. You know the importance of being able to think on your feet in your present or future career. But how do you learn to do that in a course where the instructor frames all the problems and does most of the talking? You'd also like

Service learning provides a framework for meaningful civic engagement.

to improve your public speaking skills, but will in-class presentations provide you with the practice you need? And what about writing and time management—not just for your classes but for the "real world"? For many students, service learning means not only learning about things but also learning how to do them. It supplements theories and ideas with concrete personal experience, and in doing so it helps students learn how to act on their knowledge and put theory to the test. Hence it is an especially effective way to develop critical thinking skills.

Engaging with the External Community

"Civic engagement" is participation in activities to improve your community, region, or the nation. For example, working to register new voters is a form of civic engagement.

In February 2003, a group of Oklahoma students issued what they called a "Civic Engagement Resolution." In it they complained that ". . . higher education institutions do not provide adequate education and knowledge about our civic responsibilities. We often do not know how to address civic issues. Higher education's primary focus is to produce professionals, when instead they should be producing citizens." Although it has become common to criticize the younger generation as politically apathetic, surveys indicate that more young people today are engaged in community service than at any time in the past. Yet they get little

guidance on how to develop their service activities into genuine civic engagement. As the Oklahoma students point out, higher education certainly is not doing its part. Service learning speaks directly to this problem. Indeed, facilitating civic engagement is one of its most important benefits.

Service learning is one of the very few teaching and learning strategies that provides an equal opportunity to succeed to all kinds of learners—not only students who learn well from books and who are perceptive listeners, but also those who learn best through active experimentation and hands-on projects. Service learning directly addresses a question often on the tip of a student's tongue: "Why do I have to learn this?" Because service-learning experiences let students see the utility of their knowledge even as they develop it, those experiences tend to stand out as especially meaningful—and transformative.

Practical Suggestions and Useful Resources

Whether you find service-learning opportunities available to you depends in part on your college or university, in part on your academic focus, and in part on you. Although the number of campuses with service-learning programs has grown tremendously over the last few years, many offer only traditional classroom learning with internships "on the side." Furthermore, faculty interest still varies greatly across areas of concentration. Many professors in the social sciences—in disciplines such as sociology, psychology, and communication studies—now include in their courses at least the option of doing a service-learning project. The same is true of professors in education, the health care disciplines, and social work.

If you find willing instructors and appropriate courses, you should make sure that what you are being offered is the real thing: an opportunity to reflect and discuss as well as to act; a chance to develop citizenship as well as professional skills. Remember the distinctions we considered, and don't confuse service learning with ordinary community service tacked on to a class or with internships that have simply been relabeled. If your school has a service-learning office, it can help you find faculty who understand how to design a valuable service-learning experience. Even if your school doesn't have such an office, you can easily do a little research on your own.

Community

▶▶▶ BUILDING YOUR PORTFOLIO

It's a Small World After All!

Studying abroad in Granada, Spain, was a digestive process.
The world swallowed me whole. It stripped me of everything I once knew
and assumed, and spit me out. The outcome wasn't a whole
new person, it was an open slate in which everything I now see and
hear is digested in a whole new manner that can't be explained but
only experienced by traveling abroad.

–Julie Santos, student, Global & International Studies Program, University of California, Santa Barbara

Reading about diversity, ethnicity, culture, and multiculturalism is one thing, but really stepping into someone else's shoes is another. Study abroad and student exchange programs are an excellent (and fun) way of adding new perspectives to your college experience. What better way of learning about other parts of the world than immersing yourself in a foreign culture, language, and people!

Consider the possibilities:

1. Create a new entry in your portfolio with the title "A Small World." Record your work for this assignment there.

2. Visit your institution's International Programs/Study Abroad office, or, if you are at a college that does not have a study abroad program, search for study abroad opportunities on the web.

Tip: Look for The Center for Global Education (www.globaled.us) or the Council on International Education Exchange (http://ciee.org/study.aspx).

3. Using a major or career that you selected or are interested in, think about how you would like to spend a summer, semester, or year abroad to learn more about or gain experience in your major field.

BUILDING YOUR PORTFOLIO

4. Based on your research, create a PowerPoint presentation to share with your class, outlining the opportunities to study abroad or participate in an exchange program.

   a. Describe the steps students need to take at your campus to include a study abroad trip in their college plan (e.g., who to contact, financial aid, the best time to study abroad, earning course credit.)

   b. Describe the benefits of study abroad (e.g., observing different cultures, good resume builder).

   c. Include photos of the country or countries you would like to visit.

   d. Include information about your current or intended major and career and how a study abroad or exchange trip would fit into your plans.

   e. Reference web links you found useful in preparing your presentation.

5. Attach your PowerPoint presentation to your portfolio entry.

Making the Right Choices for Your Major and Career:

Planning Early and Keeping an Open Mind

© Doug Menuez/PhotoDisc Green/Getty Images

You don't have to be sure about your academic and career goals as you begin or return to college. Rather, you can use your first classes, and even your first year, to explore your interests and see how they might connect to various academic programs. You may discover interests and opportunities you never imagined.

Depending on your academic strengths, you can major in almost anything. As this step will emphasize, it is how you integrate classes with extracurricular pursuits and work experience that prepares you for a first career—or, if you have been in the labor force for some time, for advancement in your current job or even a new career. Try a major you think you'll like, and see what develops. But keep an open mind, and don't pin all your hopes on finding a career in that major alone. Selecting a major and a career ultimately has to fit with your overall life goals, purposes, values, and beliefs. ■

In this step you will learn:

- how changes in the workplace that have occurred in your lifetime will affect how you should prepare for a career

- what personal qualities and skills are essential for career success in the information age

- what personal factors affect career choices

- how you can explore your personal interests as a path to identifying potential career choices

- how you can build a winning résumé and write a persuasive cover letter

- what you should do to prepare for a job interview

- what programs and activities are available for getting on-the-job experience and helping you land a job in your chosen career

How Do You Measure Up?

Making the Right Choices for Your Major and Career

Check the following items that apply to you:

____ 1. I realize that it's important to select a major that I feel passionate about.

____ 2. I know the entry requirements for the major or majors that interest me.

____ 3. I have a good idea of the skills I'll need to succeed in any career.

____ 4. I know about the campus resources that will help me learn about careers.

____ 5. I have begun to consider which careers match my abilities and lifestyle preferences.

____ 6. I know the importance of networking with others who can help me attain my career goals.

____ 7. I participate in out-of-class activities that relate to my career goals.

____ 8. I know how to prepare a strong résumé.

____ 9. I understand how to write an effective cover letter to accompany my résumé.

____ 10. I know how to perform well in an interview.

Review the items you did not check. Paying attention to all these aspects of your college experience can be very important to your success. After reading this step, come back to this list and choose an item or two that you did not check but are willing to work on.

Philip Gardner of Michigan State University contributed his valuable and considerable expertise to the writing of this section.

Preparing for a Career in the Information Economy

In your lifetime, companies have restructured and taken new forms to remain competitive. As a result, dramatic changes have occurred in how we work, where we work, and the ways we prepare for work while in college. The following characteristics define the economy of the early twenty-first century.

Global Increasingly, national economies have gone multinational, meaning that they not only have moved into overseas markets but also are seeking cheaper labor, capital, and resources abroad. Factories around the world built to similar standards can turn out essentially the same products. Your career is bound to be affected by the global economy, even if you never leave the United States. Many jobs that used to be based in the U.S., even those that require a high level of skill and training, are now being outsourced to other countries. For example, if you go into the hospital to have an x-ray, that x-ray may be read by radiologists in India.

Innovative The economy depends on creativity in new products and services to generate consumer interest around the world. We are witnessing an unprecedented expansion of entrepreneurial businesses that have become the foundation for new job growth.

Boundaryless Teams of workers within an organization need to understand the missions of other teams because they most likely will have to work together. U.S.-based companies have partners throughout the world. DaimlerChrysler, the result of a merger of the U.S. Chrysler organization with Germany's Mercedes-Benz group, is one example. Crossing boundaries has other implications, too. For example, you may be an accountant but find yourself working with the public relations division of your company, or you may be a human resources manager who does training for a number of different divisions in a number of different countries. You might even find yourself sometimes moving laterally—say, to a unit with a different function—rather than steadily climbing up the career ladder.

Customized More and more, consumers are demanding products and services tailored to their specific needs. For example, you surely have noticed the seemingly endless varieties of a single brand of shampoo or cereal crowding supermarket shelves. Such market segmentation requires a constant adaptation of ideas to identify new products and services as new customer demands emerge.

Fast When computers first became popular, people rejoiced because they believed the new technology would

© Photos.com/Photolibrary USA

Worker teams are a fixture in the global economy.

reduce their workloads. But rather than reducing workloads, technology has created a shift in who does certain kinds of work. Whereas assistants and other support workers once performed many tasks for executives, now executives are designing their own PowerPoint presentations because, as one article put it, "it's more fun to work with a slide show than to write reports." For better or worse, "we need it now" is the cry in the workplace, with product and service delivery time cut to a minimum (the "just-in-time" policy). Being fast requires thinking constantly outside the lines to identify new approaches to designing and delivering products.

Unstable Subprime loans, the war in Iraq, scandals within the highest ranks of major corporations, and even natural disasters have caused major fluctuations in the stock market and caused significant layoffs. Increases in oil prices have a ripple effect through many sectors of the economy. It's important to follow the economic trends, especially in times like these.

According to *Fast Company* magazine, the new information economy has changed many of the rules about work. Leaders are now expected to teach and encourage others as well as to head up their divisions. Careers frequently zigzag into other areas. People who can be one step ahead of the marketplace are in demand.

Change has become the norm. Workers are being urged to continue their learning, and companies are volunteering to play a critical role in the welfare of all people through sponsorship of worthy causes. With the lines between work and life blurring, workers need to find a healthy balance in their lives. Bringing work home may be inevitable at times, but it shouldn't be the rule.

As you work, you'll be continually enhancing and expanding your skills and competencies. You can do so on your own by taking advantage of continuing education opportunities or by attending conferences and workshops.

Essential Qualities and Skills for the Information Age

In addition to being well educated and savvy about the realities of the twenty-first-century information

TRY IT! Thinking about a Career Choice

List your personal interests, preferences, characteristics, strengths, and skills. Match your list to what you believe to be the skills and interests of successful people in a field that interests you. Note other influences that may be drawing you to that career (such as your parents' preferences). Share the notes you have prepared with a career counselor, and get feedback on how you and your career interests mesh.

economy, you'll also need a wide range of qualities and skills to succeed in your career, such as:

- communication skills that demonstrate strong oral and listening abilities, in addition to a good foundation in the basic skill of writing
- presentation skills, including the ability to justify and persuade as well as to respond to questions and serious critiques of your presentation material
- leadership skills and the ability to take charge or relinquish control, according to the needs of the organization
- team skills—the ability to work cooperatively and collaboratively with different people while maintaining autonomous control over some assignments
- interpersonal abilities that allow you to relate to others, inspire others to participate, and resolve conflict between people
- positive personal traits, including initiative and motivation, adaptability to change, a work ethic, reliability, honesty, integrity, the know-how to plan and organize multiple tasks, and the ability to respond positively to customer concerns
- critical thinking and problem solving—the ability to identify problems and their solutions by integrating information from a variety of sources and effectively weighing alternatives
- a willingness to learn quickly and continuously from those with whom you work and others around the world

Choices

Taking an **Informed** Approach to Your **Major and Career** Choices

Connecting Your Major and Your Interests with Your Career

Some students enter college knowing what they want to major in. But many others are at a loss. Some feel pressure from their families or friends to select or reject certain majors. Some students even select majors and careers on the basis of how a certain career is portrayed on TV or in the movies. Remember that, ultimately, the decision about an academic major and career is your decision.

Before you decide, consider your interests, abilities, and lifestyle preferences. It's also a good idea to gain real-world experience by experimenting with your chosen career through internships, co-ops, or shadowing someone in the profession. When you shadow someone, you observe that person in his or her professional activities over several days or weeks. Your academic adviser can help you understand entry requirements for the major that interests you and can assist you in gaining the insight you need to make the right choice.

At some point you'll probably ask yourself, "Why am I in college?" If you are like many students, you may respond, "So I can get a good job or an education for a specific career." The problem with this answer is that most majors do not lead into a specific career path or job. In fact, you can enter most career paths from any number of academic majors.

Marketing, a common undergraduate business major, is a field that recruits from a wide variety of majors, including advertising, communications, and psychology. Sociology majors find jobs in law enforcement, teaching, and public service. English majors are designing web pages, and history majors are sales representatives and business managers. You do not have to major in science to gain admittance to medical school. You do have to take the required science and math courses, but medical schools seek applicants with diverse backgrounds. Only a few technical or professional fields, such as accounting, nursing, and engineering, are tied to specific majors.

Nursing is a popular major today.

© PhotoDisc Red/Getty Images

To explore your reasons for coming to college, ask yourself:

- "Am I here to find out who I am and study a subject I'm truly passionate about, regardless of whether it leads to the career I planned?"
- "Am I here to engage in an academic program that provides an array of possibilities when I graduate?"
- "Am I here to prepare myself for a graduate program?"
- "Am I here to obtain specific training in a field that I'm committed to?"
- "Am I here to gain specific skills for a job I already have?"

In your interactions with academic advisers and career counselors, let them know your specific reasons for coming to college and your plans for applying your college education in the future. With this information, they can help you make better decisions.

Career Choice as a Process of Discovery

Students frequently encounter bumps along the road toward planning and achieving their career goals. Choosing a career is a process of discovery, involving a willingness to remain open to new ideas and experiences. Why should you begin thinking about

Choices

your career early in your college experience? Because many of the decisions you make during your first year will have an impact on where you end up in the workplace.

As you think about your career, also consider that:

You are, more or less, solely responsible for your career. At one time, organizations provided structured "ladders" employees could climb to advance to higher professional levels. In most cases, such ladders have disappeared. Companies may assist you with assessments and information on available positions in the industry, but the ultimate task of engineering a career path is yours.

To advance your career, you must accept the risks that accompany employment and plan for the future. Organizations continually restructure, merge, and either grow or downsize in response to economic conditions. As a result, positions may be cut. Because you can be unexpectedly unemployed, keep other career options in mind as you take courses.

A college degree does not guarantee employment. As a college graduate, you'll be able to pursue opportunities that are more rewarding, financially and otherwise, than if you did not have a degree. But simply wanting to work in a certain field or for a certain organization doesn't mean there will always be a job for you there. Be flexible when exploring your career options; you may have begun your work life in a job that is not exactly in line with your major or career goals.

A commitment to lifelong learning will help keep you employable. In your college courses you are learning a vital skill: how to learn. Actually, your learning has just begun when you receive your diploma.

Now the good news: Thousands of graduates find jobs every year. Some may have to work longer to get where they want to be, but persistence pays off. If you start now, you'll have time to build a portfolio of academic and cocurricular experiences that will add substance to your career profile.

The knowledge to manage your career comes from you (why, who, how) and from an understanding of your career objectives (what, where, when):

Why Why do you want to be a _____? Knowing your goals and values will help you pursue your career with passion and an understanding of what motivates you.

Who Network with people who can help you find out what you want to be. Right now, that might be a professor in your major, an academic adviser, or someone at your campus career center. Later, network with others who can help you attain your goal.

How Develop the technical and communications skills required to work effectively. Become an expert with computer programs such as PowerPoint and Excel. Learn to build web pages. Improve your writing skills. Even if you think your ideal job doesn't require these skills, you'll be more marketable with them.

What Be aware of the opportunities an employer presents, as well as such potential threats as outsourcing—a company's hiring of outside businesses to perform certain core tasks. Understand the employment requirements for the career field you have chosen. Know what training you will need to remain in your chosen profession.

Where Know the points of entry into the field. For example, you can obtain valuable hands-on experience through internships, co-ops, or part-time jobs that can help you get a full-time job in your field of interest.

When Know how early you need to start looking for the job you want. Find out if certain professions hire at certain times of the year.

Exploring Your Interests

John Holland, a psychologist at Johns Hopkins University, has developed tools and concepts that can help you organize the various dimensions of yourself so that you can identify potential career choices and choose your major. Holland separates people into six general categories on the basis of differences in their interests, skills, values, and personality characteristics—in short, their preferred approaches to life.[1]

The Holland Model: Personality Characteristics

Realistic (R) These people describe themselves as concrete, down-to-earth, and practical doers. They exhibit competitive/assertive behavior and show interest in activities that require motor coordination, skill, and physical strength. They prefer situations involving action solutions rather than tasks involving verbal or interpersonal skills, and they like to take a concrete approach to problem solving rather than rely on abstract theory. They tend to be interested in scientific or mechanical areas rather than cultural and aesthetic fields.

Investigative (I) These people describe themselves as analytical, rational, and logical problem solvers. They value intellectual stimulation and intellectual achievement and prefer to think rather than to act, to organize and understand rather than to persuade. They usually have a strong interest in physical, biological, or social sciences. They are less likely to be people oriented.

Artistic (A) These people describe themselves as creative, innovative, and independent. They value self-expression and relations with others through artistic expression and are also emotionally expressive. They dislike structure, preferring tasks involving personal or physical skills. They resemble investigative people but are more interested in the cultural or the aesthetic than the scientific.

Social (S) These people describe themselves as kind, caring, helpful, and understanding of others. They value helping and making a contribution. They satisfy their needs in one-on-one or small-group interaction using strong speaking skills to teach, counsel, or advise. They are drawn to close interpersonal relationships and are less likely to engage in intellectual or extensive physical activity.

Enterprising (E) These people describe themselves as assertive, risk taking, and persuasive. They value prestige, power, and status and are more inclined than other types to pursue it. They use verbal skills to supervise, lead, direct, and persuade rather than to support or guide. They are interested in people and in achieving organizational goals.

Conventional (C) These people describe themselves as neat, orderly, detail oriented, and persistent. They value order, structure, prestige, and status and possess a high degree of self-control. They are not opposed to rules and regulations. They are skilled in organizing, planning, and scheduling and are interested in data and people.

The Holland Model: Career Fields

Holland's system organizes career fields into the same six categories. Career fields are grouped according to what a particular career field requires of a person (skills and personality characteristics most commonly associated with success in those fields) and what rewards those fields provide (interests and values most commonly associated with satisfaction). Here are a few examples.

Realistic (R) Agricultural engineer, electrical contractor, industrial arts teacher, navy officer, fitness director, packaging engineer, electronics technician, computer graphics technician

Investigative (I) Urban planner, chemical engineer, bacteriologist, flight engineer, genealogist, laboratory technician, marine scientist, nuclear medicine technologist, obstetrician, quality-control technician, computer programmer, environmentalist, physician, college professor

Artistic (A) Architect, film editor/director, actor, cartoonist, interior decorator, fashion model, graphic communications specialist, journalist, editor, orchestra leader, public relations specialist, sculptor, media specialist, librarian, reporter

Social (S) Nurse, teacher, social worker, genetic counselor, marriage counselor, rehabilitation counselor,

---

[1]Adapted from John L. Holland, *Self-Directed Search Manual* (Odessa, FL: Psychological Assessment Resources, 1985).

Choices

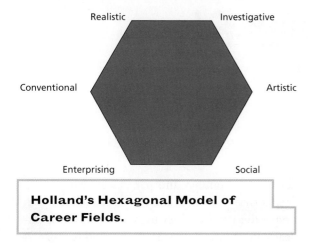

school superintendent, geriatric specialist, insurance claims specialist, minister, travel agent, guidance counselor, convention planner

Enterprising (E) Banker, city manager, FBI agent, health administrator, judge, labor arbitrator, salary and wage administrator, insurance salesperson, sales engineer, lawyer, sales representative, marketing specialist

Conventional (C) Accountant, statistician, census enumerator, data processor, hospital administrator, insurance administrator, office manager, underwriter, auditor, personnel specialist, database manager, abstractor/indexer

Your career choices ultimately will involve a complex assessment of the factors most important to you. To display the relationship between career fields and the potential conflicts people face as they consider them, Holland's model is commonly presented in a hexagonal shape (see figure). The closer the types, the closer the relationships among the career fields; the farther apart the types, the more conflict between the career fields.

Holland's model can help you address the problem of career choice in two ways. First, you can begin to identify many career fields that are consistent with what you know about yourself. Once you've identified potential fields, you can use the career library at your college to get more information about those fields, such as daily activities for specific jobs, interests and abilities required, preparation required for entry, working conditions, salary and benefits, and employment outlook. Second, you can begin to identify the harmony or conflicts in your career choices. This will help you to analyze the reasons for your career decisions and to be more confident as you make choices.

Never feel you have to make a decision simply on the basis of the results of one assessment. Career choices are complex and involve many factors; furthermore, these decisions are not irreversible. Take time to talk your interests over with a career counselor. Another helpful approach is to shadow an individual in the occupation that interests you, to obtain an "in the trenches" understanding of what the occupation entails in terms of skills, commitment, and opportunity.

Factors Affecting Career Choices

Some people have a definite self-image when they enter college, but most of us are still in the process of defining (and redefining) ourselves throughout life. We can look at ourselves in several useful ways with respect to possible careers:

- **Values.** Today, more than ever, knowing your core values (your most important beliefs) will be important in shaping your career path. In a fast economy, having a strong rudder will help you steer through the turbulent times.
- **Interests.** Interests develop from your experiences and beliefs and can continue to develop and change throughout life. You may be interested in writing for the college newspaper because you wrote for your high school paper. It's not unusual to enter Psych 101 with a great interest in psychology and realize halfway through the course that psychology is not what you imagined.
- **Skills.** Skills, or the ability to do something well, can usually be improved with practice.
- **Aptitudes.** Aptitudes, the foundation for skills, are inherent strengths that are often part of your biological heritage or the result of early training. We each have aptitudes we can build on. Build on your strengths.
- **Personality.** Your personality makes you *you* and can't be ignored when you make career decisions. The quiet, orderly, calm, detail-oriented person probably will make a different work choice than the aggressive, outgoing, "big picture" person.
- **Life goals and work values.** Each of us defines success and satisfaction in our own way. The process is complex and very personal. Two factors influence our conclusions about success and happiness: (1) knowing that we are achieving the life goals we've set for ourselves, and (2) finding that we gain satisfaction from what we're receiving from our work. If your values are in conflict with the organizational values where you work, you may be in for trouble.

Setting Your Career Plan in Motion

When the time comes to apply for a job that interests you, you'll want to know the best strategies for success. To prepare, take advantage of campus and online resources that will help you shape a winning résumé, write a persuasive cover letter, and excel in the interview. Also find out about the many programs that are available to give you experience and a taste of the day-to-day realities of jobs in your dream career.

Building a Résumé

Before you finish college, you'll need a résumé—whether it's for a part-time job, for an internship, or for a co-op position.

A résumé may be chronological, or it may be organized by skills. As a rule, you'll probably opt for the chronological résumé, which lists your work experience from the most recent to the earliest. But you may decide on the skills résumé if you can group skills from a number of jobs under meaningful categories. Aim for one page, but if you have many outstanding things to say, add a second page.

Writing a Cover Letter

When you are sending a cover letter to a prospective employer, the following steps are essential:

- **Find out whom to write to.** It's not the same in all fields. If you were seeking a marketing position at an advertising agency, you would write to the director of account services. If you were approaching General Motors about an engineering position, you might write to a special human resources director in charge of engineering. Your academic adviser or career counselor can help you. Never write "To whom it may concern."
- **Get the most recent name and address.** Your adviser or career counselor can guide you to references in your campus or career library.
- **Use the proper format for the date, address, and salutation.** The person reading your letter will want to see if you pay attention to details.

Getting Experience

Once you have a good sense of your interests, test the waters and do some career exploration. Your campus

© Jupiterimages/Comstock/Alamy

has a variety of activities and programs in which you can participate to confirm those interests, check your values, and gain valuable skills. These include:

Service learning/volunteering Some instructors build service learning into their courses. Service learning allows you to apply academic theories and ideas to actual practice. Volunteering outside of class is also a valuable way to encounter different life situations and to gain work knowledge in various areas, such as teaching, health services, and counseling.

Study abroad Spend at least one term taking courses in another country. Learn to adapt to new traditions and a different pace of life. Some study abroad programs also include options for both work and service learning experiences.

Internships and co-ops Many employers want to see that you have experience in the workplace and an understanding of the skills necessary to succeed. Check with your academic department and your career center on available internships in your major. Many majors offer academic credit for internships.

On-campus employment On-campus jobs give you a chance to practice good work habits. On-campus employment also brings you into contact with faculty and other academic professionals whom you can later consult or ask for references.

Research An excellent way to extend your academic learning is to work with a faculty member on a research project. Research extends your critical thinking skills and provides insight on a subject above and beyond your books and class notes.

Interviewing

The first year of college may not seem like a time to be concerned about interviews. However, students often find themselves in interview situations shortly after arriving on campus: vying for positions on the student residence governing board, applying for a job, competing for a second-year scholarship, applying to be a residence hall assistant, and pursuing an opportunity to be an intern or a research assistant.

The purpose of the interview is to exchange information. The interviewers' goal is to evaluate your abilities and competencies. You, on the other hand, are looking for a match between your interests and abilities and the position you are seeking.

Here are some important interviewing tips:

- Check with your career counselor to see if you can attend a mock interview. Usually designed for graduating students as they prep for their on-campus interviews, mock interviews help students strategize and feel comfortable with an interview. If a mock interview session is not available, the career center will have tips for handling an interview situation.
- In a behavioral interview, the interviewer assumes that your past experiences are good predictors of your future abilities and performance. He or she wants to hear about your accomplishments that can help in the assessment of your skills and behaviors. One useful approach to answering behavioral questions is the PARK method, focusing on P, the problem or situation you faced; A, the actions you took; R, the results or outcomes of your actions; and K, the knowledge you gained and applied through the experience.
- Dress appropriately. Dress conventions vary depending on the location of the interview and the type of interview (professional, student-focused). First impressions matter, so it is better to dress too professionally (in a dress suit and polished shoes) than too informally.

Where to Go for Help: Choosing and Pursuing a Major and a Career

ON CAMPUS

Career center: Almost every college campus has a career center where you can obtain free counseling and information. Career professionals will help you define your interests. They will also interpret results of any assessment you complete, coach you on interviewing, and critique your résumé.

Academic advising: More and more advisers have been trained in what is known as "developmental advising," or helping you look beyond individual classes to a career search. Talking to your adviser is often the best place to start. If you have not declared a major, your adviser may be able to help you with that decision as well.

Faculty: On many campuses, faculty members actively help students connect academic interests to careers. Faculty in professional curricula, such as business and other applied fields, often have direct contact with companies and serve as contacts for internships.

Upper-class students: Students farther along in college can help you navigate courses and find important resources. They may also have practical experience from internships and volunteering.

ONLINE

Occupational Information Network: http://online.onecenter.org. This federal government site has information on occupations, skill sets, and links to professional sites for selected occupations. This is a great place to get started thinking about your interests.

Mapping Your Future: www.mappingyourfuture.biz. This comprehensive site provides support for those who are just starting their career explorations.

For help with resume writing and building: **http://jobsearchtech.about.com/**

WIRED WINDOW

IN ADDITION TO CHECKING your resume and references, potential employers will also use online resources to learn more about you. In a recent national survey of college employers, slightly more than 11 percent said that they review candidate profiles on social networking sites like MySpace and Facebook and more than 60 percent said that the information they find has at least some influence on their hiring decisions. Since a user outside of your Facebook network cannot see your profile, companies have asked their employees who are recent graduates or their college interns to research potential candidates. On profile pages, employers can find discrepancies between a candidate's resume and their actual academic and work experience. Potential employers might even spot other kinds of information or see pictures that would make them think twice about hiring you. Keep in mind that most of the people making hiring decisions at companies don't understand social networking websites the way you do—they are wary of

sharing any personal information online. When they find that a potential candidate is comfortable sharing his or her party pictures, describing personal escapades that some might consider inappropriate, or allowing friends to post crude comments, they will seriously question the judgment of that applicant. Knowing this, what would you change about your Facebook and/or MySpace profile to make it more appropriate for viewing by potential employers?

Now that you know what employers are looking for when they search social networking websites to research potential employees, pretend you are an employer. Pick either Facebook or MySpace and search for your friends—what did you find? How many of your friends would you hire based solely on their profile page? How many would you not hire based on the information or pictures on their profile page? Why? What about your own profile? What would a potential employer find there, and how might he or she react?

▶▶▶ BUILDING YOUR PORTFOLIO

Investigating Occupations

The best career advice to give to the young is
"Find out what you like doing best and get
someone to pay you for doing it."
–Katherine Whitehorn (b. 1926), British writer and journalist

How do you know how to select a major if you are not sure what you want to do when you graduate? College classes, out-of-class activities, and part-time jobs will help you narrow your choices and make decisions about a major and a potential career.

1. Create a new entry in your portfolio with the title, "Investigating Occupations." Record your work for this assignment there.

2. List at least two majors that you are considering right now or that you would like to know more about. Why do you find these majors interesting?

3. What are two careers that you think you might be interested in after you graduate? Explain your answer.

4. The U.S. Bureau of Labor Statistics publishes the online *Occupational Outlook Handbook*, which provides details for hundreds of jobs. You can search for a specific job and learn about the training and education needed, median earnings, job prospects, roles and responsibilities on the job, and working conditions.

    a. Visit the *Occupational Outlook Handbook* online at **www.bls.gov/oco** and type the first career name that you listed above in the search field.

    b. Look through the search results to find the specific career that you are interested in learning more about.

    c. In the chart below, note the training/degree required, describe the job outlook, and list the median earnings for each career. Look through the other descriptions to learn more about the career.

Even in your first year of college it is important that you begin to think about what you are going to do after graduation. The more you investigate different types of careers, the easier it will be for you to identify a major or help you decide what kind of internship, part-time job, or service learning opportunity you want to experience while you are still in college. Exploring your strengths, interests, and goals will help you to find a career that you enjoy and that meets your lifestyle expectations.

Source: Used by permission of Career Passport, Michigan State University. (Adapted.)

Credits

Text Credits

College 7: Finding a Mentor, D. J. Levinson et al., *The Seasons of a Man's Life* (NY: Ballantine, 1978).

Think 26: Thinking Critically: Searching beyond Right and Wrong, Theodora J. Kalikow, "Misconceptions about the Word 'Liberal' in Liberal Arts Education," Higher Education and National Affairs, June 8, 1998; 28–29: Collaboration Fosters Critical Thinking, Anuradha Gokhale, "Collaborative Learning Enhances Critical Thinking," *Journal of Technology Education* 7, no. 1 (1995); 34: Critically Evaluating Information on the Internet, Adapted from Robert Harris. "Evaluating Internet Research Sources." VirtualSalt. 17 Nov. 1997 from http://www.virtualsalt.com/evalu8it.htm. Reprinted by permission.

Learn 40: Collaborative Learning Teams, Joseph Cuseo, *Igniting Student Involvement, Peer Interaction, and Teamwork: A Taxonomy of Specific Cooperative Learning Structures and Collaborative Learning Strategies,* Stillwater, OK: New Forum Press (2002); 44–45: The VARK Questionnaire, © Copyright Version 5.1 (2004) held by Neil D. Fleming, Christchurch, New Zealand and Charles C. Bonwell, Green Mountain Falls, Colorado 80819 U.S.A.

Clearly 54–55: The Power of Writing, William Zinsser, *On Writing Well* (New York: Harper Resource 25th Anniversary Edition, 2001), 53: Finding a Topic, Robert Pirsig, *Zen and the Art of Motorcycle Maintenance* (New York: Bantam Books, 1984); 56: Allocating Time for Each Writing Stage, Donald Murray, *Learning by Teaching: Selected Articles on Writing and Teaching* (Portsmouth, NH: Boynton/ Cook, 1982), 57: Lynne Truss, *Eats, Shoots & Leaves: The Zero Tolerance Approach to Punctuation* (New York: Gotham Books, 2003); 57: Mastering E-Mail: Another Method of Communication, Kaitlin Duck Sherwood, "A Beginner's Guide to Effective E-mail," http://www.webfoot.com/advice/email.top.html; 59: Speaking on the Sport, Kenneth Wydro, *Think on Your Feet* (Englewood Cliffs, NJ: Prentice-Hall, 1981).

Relate 108–109: Types of Values, M. Rokeach, *Understanding Human Values: Individual and Societal* (New York: The Free Press, 1979).

Health 113: Promoting Your Sexual Health, "National College Health Risk Behavior Study,"Centers for Disease Control and Prevention (2005); 119: Tobacco—The Other Legal Drug, CDC, "Prevalence of Current Cigarette Smoking among Adults and Change in Prevalence of Current and Some Day Smoking— United States, 1996–2000," *Morbidity and Mortality Weekly Report* 52, no. 14 (April 2003): 303–7; 119: Tobacco—The Other Legal Drug, Rigotti, N., Lee, J. and Wechsler, H. "U.S. College Students' Use of Tobacco Products: Results of a National Survey." *Journal of the American Medical Association* 284:6 (2000): 699–705; 120: Stimulants, Adapted from "Prescription Drugs: Abuse and Addiction." National Institute on Drug Abuse, part of the National Institutes of Health (NIH), a division of the U.S. Department of Health and Human Services (DHHS) (2001); 121: Anabolic Steroids, "2004 Monitoring the Future Survey," funded by the National Institute on Drug Abuse, National Institutes of Health, DHHS, and conducted by the University of Michigan's Institute for Social Research; 121: Ecstasy, Excerpted from "Ecstasy: What We Know and Don't Know About MDMA: A Scientific Review." National Institute on Drug Abuse, part of the NIH, a division of the DHHS (2004).

Choices 142: Exploring Your Interests, Reproduced by special permission of the Publisher, Psychological Assessment Resources, Inc., 16204 North Florida Avenue, Lutz, Florida 33549, from the Self-Directed Search Professional's User's Guide by John L. Holland, Ph.D., Copyright 1985, 1987, 1994, 1997, Further reproduction is prohibited without permission from PAR, Inc.; 143: Holland's Hexagonal Model of Career Fields, Reproduced by special permission of the Publisher, Psychological Assessment Resources, Inc., 16204 North Florida Avenue, Lutz, Florida 33549, from the Self-Directed Search Professional's User's Guide by John L. Holland, Ph.D., Copyright 1985, 1987,

Photo Credits

Index

V

Value dualisms, 132
Values, 100–101, 108, 132
VARK learning style, 44–46,
    50–51
Visual aids, in public speaking, 61
Visual learning, 44, 47, 78. *See also*
    VARK learning style
Vocabulary, 81

Voice, 58–59
Volunteer learning, 144

W

Wellness, 112
Wheel map, 78
Wikipedia, 62
Wired Window. *See* technology

Write learning, 44, 47. *See also* VARK
    learning style
Writing, 52–57
Writing center, 12, 59

Z

Zinsser, William, 54–55